Arroz con Pollo
and Apple Pie:

Raising Bicultural Children

Maritere Rodriguez Bellas

Arroz con Pollo and Apple Pie

www.maritererodriguezbellas.com

First printing, 2016

Interior design and formatting by The Write Assistants

Table of Contents

iv

"Raising a family away from your home country is not easy. Raising a family in a different culture, while trying to preserve your own roots and traditions, is a difficult task. And what about trying to keep your mother language alive at home? So challenging for many. I know this, because I've been there. But we shouldn't have to choose between a culture or another, a language or the other, because, just like Mrs. Bellas shows us in this book, it's possible to raise children who are proud of their bicultural heritage. With sound advice and born from life experience, Maritere Bellas offers us pragmatic, down-to-earth solutions and tips to make the most out of our bi-cultural experience. *Arroz con Pollo and Apple Pie* is a must read for all families raising first generation Americans with Latino flavor."

-Mariana Llanos, author, bilingual childrens' books

"As an immigrant from El Salvador, I know firsthand what it is like to have to adjust to living with two cultures and languages in a new country. Maritere's book is a must read for immigrant parents living in the United States."

- René Colato Laínez, author, children's multicultural picture books

Foreword

More than 200 million people in the world live in a place other than where they were born. However impressive the number, it does not fully describe the complex and often difficult process of adapting to a new place and the survival strategies individuals use to make it from day to day until they can function successfully in this new setting.

The process of migration adaptation has been looked at in terms of how many migrants obtain good jobs, increase their incomes, and obtain citizenship. The most important adaptation measure missing from the list is how well parents are able to help their children adapt to a life in the country of destination, while their own lives continue to be linked to their countries of origin. Parents who can accomplish this goal are likely to provide their children with opportunities unavailable to themselves and to adapt better themselves as they seek out ways to help their children.

This book provides insights into the lives of Latino families who have faced and managed to find solutions to help their children succeed in their adopted country. Readers can learn valuable lessons from these family stories. Immigrant parents in particular will fully understand the common situations presented in each chapter of the book and be able to reflect on their own successes.

Dr. Leo Estrada, Ph.D.
Luskin School of Public Affairs
University of California, Los Angeles

Introduction

My son was a baby when I first had the idea of writing a book for immigrant parents. I was living in California and had no family there, except my husband. I desperately needed advice and guidance. Whenever I needed to talk to someone about the baby, I called my sister in Puerto Rico, but that was an expensive routine which I couldn't keep up for long. It was hard being alone. I had grown up in a very close family and never imagined I would not be living near them when I became a mother. I missed my mom, my dad, my sister and my brothers. Having no parenting experience, I went to the library and the bookstore, but there were no parenting books for the Latino immigrant mother. In fact, at the time, there were no online resources that could help with my parenting questions.

Don't get me wrong. Parents have instincts and common sense, regardless of where they reside or the culture in which they were raised. But being away from home, away from where I grew up and away from everything I knew and loved, made parenting especially difficult. After all, my baby wasn't going to stay a baby for long, and then I would have to raise him within two cultures. How would I do that?

When my daughter was born, my mother came to stay with us. After five weeks, she had to go back home, and I was left to raise two kids with two sets of cultural values. Once again, I asked myself, *"How am I going to do this?"*

For years, I wondered if I was doing the right thing as a parent, given that my children's bicultural values often clashed with my own. My husband told me to think of all the immigrant mothers who faced even more challenges than I: no husband, no English language skills, little education, strenuous jobs (often more than one), or perhaps no job at all. A seed was planted in my mind: I wanted to do something to help other Latino immigrant parents.

To that end, I contacted my friend Monica Lozano at *La Opinión*, the largest Spanish language newspaper in the country and suggested a parenting column for the Latino immigrant parent. She supported the idea and my column ran in the paper for eleven years. By the time my kids were in school, I was determined to write a book for the immigrant parent. Fast-forward fifteen years: the book you are holding in your hands is the one I needed when my kids were born, which I hope you'll find helpful as you navigate parenting in a country that you may often find baffling.

Arroz Con Pollo and Apple Pie is written for the immigrant parent who is grappling with a uniquely challenging set of dilemmas. You are part of a rapidly growing segment of the U.S. population who desperately want to guide their children, so they can fulfill the American dream and preserve Latino values. Whether you are Mexican, Cuban, Salvadorian, Peruvian, Guatemalan, Argentine or Puerto Rican, this book will help you make decisions in a culture vastly different than the one in which you grew up.

Arroz Con Pollo and Apple Pie is designed to offer strategies, tips, and solutions, as well as compelling stories of how other immigrant families deal or have dealt with the same issues you are grappling with: the adjustment to the new life and raising children with two cultures. You will read stories about people like Candy from Nicaragua and how she came to the United States, leaving her older son behind, their struggle to reunite, what it was like when he finally came, and how the family had to learn to adjust to being together again as she faced the challenge of raising him with two cultures. Margarita's story is also inspiring. She came here from Mexico, alone at age fourteen, determined to learn the language and get an education. She managed to find a balance between the two cultures and became a role model as her two daughters struggled with the same issue. You'll meet young Marlon, from Guatemala, who, at age five, was separated from his mom, then came to this country as a teenager, without seeing his birth mother for almost ten years, and the challenges he went through until he finally adjusted. The final chapter offers comments by immigrant baby boomers (born between 1946-

1964) raised in this country, as well as stories of Millennials (individuals born in the early 1980s to early 2002) who were raised bilingual and bicultural, and now demonstrate the benefits and advantages in their lives. In addition, well-known Latinos—including Univision Network co-anchor, Jorge Ramos, Cuban actor, Tony Plana, and renowned Dominican singer and author, Milly Quezada—share their insights on the Latino immigrant experience and how it influenced the way they were raised and the way they raised their children. You will find some of these stories woven into each chapter. At the end of each chapter, I offer tips and suggestions in the form of questions to get you started in your quest to find balance and help your children. I also offer you a space to write your parenting journal and ask questions to get you started. For parents reading the e-book version of this book, I invite you to use the suggested prompts to start a journal of your own.

All of us who came to the U.S. from another country, regardless of our profession or economic background, have struggled to raise accomplished, happy, and well-adjusted children. It is my hope that this book will offer you a fresh look at what finding a balance between two cultures can be like. These stories I share are insightful and filled with details of what it can be like to leave everything behind and start over. In addition, I provide online resources for even more information and knowledge. As a Latina mother who has lived the immigrant experience and often felt that I was neither from here, nor from there, I welcome you to your unique parenting experience!

Maritere Rodriguez Bellas

BECOMING BICULTURAL

Chapter 1: The Stages of Immigrant Adjustment

"My husband and I had no choice. We had to come to America. We have three children, and there was little work back home, but it has been hard. Things are different here. It is a difficult adjustment."
—Rosario, age 30

Why did you immigrate to America? Was it to find work? Search for a better life for you and your family? Was it to escape the political environment in your native country? Perhaps a family member was already here and told you about the opportunities in the U.S. Most likely, your reason for moving here is a combination of the above. Regardless of the reasons, we all go through a period of adjustment in order to achieve a balance between the two cultures.

As Latino immigrants, we often arrive in the United States with preconceived ideas about the life we will find here. We may not fully anticipate the differences in cultural values, but we soon discover those distinctions. Some of us will find that the ways we are expected to think and act clash with our strongly held beliefs; others may rebel against the changes we have to make in order to fit in. For those who already have relatives here, the adjustment may be easier. Some assimilate so completely, that they seem to forget where they came from—but of course, they don't. Being an immigrant is a continuous cultural battle.

As immigrants, we must find a way to strike a comfortable balance between Latino and American values. We not only must adjust to a different set of rules and a different way of life than the ones we grew up with, but we must also oversee our children's adjustment to these new standards. Embracing a new culture does not mean that we must accept everything about it, nor does it mean that we must forget our native culture. It means that we gradually accept the reality of living within two different, but ultimately compatible worlds.

Adjustment is a process everyone goes through when moving to a new country. The stages of adjustment can happen when we first move here, or after we have been in this country a long time and finally call it our own. In many ways, the stages are similar to the grieving process. They are:

1. Confusion/Denial,
2. Disappointment/Anger,
3. Resentment,
4. And finally, Acceptance.

Let's review the stages one at a time. As you read through these stages, see if you can identify where you might fall in the progression. The lines aren't always clear-cut between stages, but the goal should be plain: to move towards the final stage of acceptance.

Confusion and Denial

In this stage, we may deny the emotional hardships we are experiencing as immigrants. We may ask ourselves, "What is the big deal? I can learn to live in a new country. I can leave my children behind for a while. I want a better life for my family, so I can put up with difficulties without feeling any distress. I can do it." Deep inside we believe we made the right choice by coming to this country, but we feel confused by our emotions. On one hand, we are relieved to be working towards a better life; on the other hand, we feel homesick, sad, or lonely. Sometimes we even refuse to be happy because that would mean forgetting where we came from.

Confusion and denial can lead to nostalgia and guilt. Nostalgia arises when we focus on what our life was like in our country of origin, rather than the possibilities that lie ahead for us here. We often idealize our past and remember things as being better back home than they really were. Sometimes we forget the reasons why we immigrated. Guilt can be part of our daily lives: guilt for leaving our parents or our children behind, guilt that we are not able to send money to our aging parents or be with them when they get sick, guilt because we do not speak the language, and guilt because we cannot find a higher paying job to provide a better life for our children.

There are immigrants who never fully accept the changes they have to make to live here. Sometimes, these people get stuck in one of these early stages. One example is the mother of my friend Erica, an Argentinian-American born in New York.

Erica's mother, who was born in Argentina, moved to the U.S. when she was an adult, and had a hard time adjusting to her new life. Erica is convinced that her mom would have preferred to live in Argentina, given the choice. After a few decades here, Erica's mom still prefers Spanish television and is still devoted to her Hispanic customs and traditions. "I just think it was hard for her to find a common ground between the two cultures," Erica said. That can happen to many immigrants. It is easier to hold on to the life we left behind at all costs.

Disappointment and Anger

Even though there are many opportunities in the United States, there are also obstacles. Perhaps English is not our first language, and it is not as easy as we thought to get by without it. Maybe the job we thought would be waiting for us did not come through. Or we get the job and then are fired because we are not able to communicate well with our employer. Things may not be as easy as our family and friends made them out to be. Whether we held a good job, or had nothing at all back in our native country, we feel less confident because we are starting over in a largely different and anonymous environment. Our disappointment leads to vulnerability, frustration, and resentment. All we see is the outside reality of other people's successes— "Gloria got a better job than me because she speaks better English," or "Lupita was able to get an interview at that hair salon because her cousin knew the owner." What we don't see is that both Gloria and Lupita had to go through the same stages of adjustments. All immigrants do, and disappointment and anger are often one of those stages.

It took Isabel, an immigrant from El Salvador, years to get past this stage, even though she had longed to come to America. Her story began when her husband left her with their three children. With political turmoil swirling around her, and jobs scarce in her home country, Isabel had trouble paying the rent. She could not buy new clothes for her children and had to walk everywhere because she could not afford a car. Although she knew it would be difficult and even dangerous, she dreamed of crossing the border and starting over in America. Isabel's sister was already there and encouraged Isabel to join her. Her children would have to stay behind with her mother, but she believed everything would work out in the long run.

Isabel had finished high school and spoke some English when she arrived from El Salvador. She knew that living in America would require an adjustment, but she did not realize how little her education would be valued here. The secretarial job she had envisioned was unattainable. Most people applying for these positions had attended college and she had not. "I felt discouraged and sad, and my self-esteem suffered," she said. Moreover, Isabel resented the lack of respect. She felt judged and patronized, and was angry about not being strong enough to stand up for herself. Women at the factory where she worked made fun of her because she wore a skirt and blouse typical of her country. "I should have said something, but I was intimidated. They made me feel so inadequate!"

She also felt frustrated when she was not given a promotion at the factory, even though she had proven herself a hard worker. "My employer did not give me the opportunity because he assumed I would be unable to delegate tasks. I was disappointed and hurt at his lack of support." That experience made her resentful, and it took her a long time to build up her confidence. Yet, her kids never knew her struggles. When she talked to them, she always sounded cheerful and kept reminding them that they would be together.

When her kids finally joined her in the U.S., Isabel had two jobs in order to make ends meet. She was so busy working that she had no time to think about how the cultural differences were impacting her family. When her kids got into trouble, however, she realized that being angry wasn't helping anyone. She knew she had to work harder on accepting her new American life. Acceptance is, of course, the final stage of adjustment.

Resentment

During the resentment stage, we live in survival mode. We tell ourselves that we have to make this transition work—and fast. So we roll up our sleeves and do whatever it takes to reach our goals, to reunite with our kids, to make our lives viable. But survival mode can make us feel resentful. Not only do we resent having to work so hard, we also resent all the changes we have to face. We even envy those who do not have to struggle as hard as we do. Then again, we assume that others don't have to struggle as much when we really don't know their story. This is part of what happened to Consuelo.

Consuelo came to the United States a few years ago from an impoverished rural town in Mexico. She joined her husband, José, who had immigrated a year earlier. Her two sons, ages ten and five, had to stay behind with their grandmother until Consuelo and José could save enough money to send for them.

When Consuelo arrived in the United States, she spoke no English, did not know how to drive a car, and had never seen a dishwasher. She had not been away from home before, not even to the capital of Mexico. "The first months here were the hardest. I spoke no English, so I felt inadequate and insecure. I cried often and constantly worried about my children. I worried that they were not being helpful or obedient to their grandmother. I worried that my children would forget me. I worried that my children would not forgive me for leaving them. I worried that I would like it here so much that I would forget them," she said.

All these feelings made her confused, but then she remembered why she was here and became determined and focused. She wanted so desperately to learn the language that she would only watch English-language television and enrolled in a night class at her church. Anything to keep her busy so she wouldn't miss her country and experience heartache. "I wanted to belong here, to feel good about coming," she said.

Everything in the U.S. was new for Consuelo. She couldn't believe all the appliances people owned. The big buildings and the paved streets awed her. Quickly, the newness gave way to disappointment. Though most everyone in the neighborhood spoke Spanish, she needed to know English to get a better job. She applied for a waitress job at two Mexican restaurants, but was turned down. "Our customers speak English," she was told. She was often turned down for housekeeping jobs because the employer didn't speak Spanish and was not able to communicate with her.

Consuelo resented her friend, Teresa, who had a well-paying job at a factory. Lorena, who was hired as a waitress in a Mexican restaurant, also made more money than Consuelo. Both Teresa and Lorena had learned English quickly when they arrived. Everything seemed harder for Consuelo. She was tired of cleaning houses and resented the lady whose house she cleaned because she was not very nice to her. Consuelo was pregnant, but her employer never showed any compassion. Still, she would shake off her feelings and move on for her own sake and the sake of her children.

Consuelo knew she had to make her life in America work, but her resentment of the struggles and inequities made things difficult for her and her family.

Acceptance

It may help you to know that a vast number of immigrants reach the acceptance stage. In this stage, we accept our new country with all of its benefits and flaws. Although we love our country of origin and value our heritage, we also acknowledge and respect the values of a country that has offered us a home and boundless opportunities.

Reaching this stage may take months or even years.

First, people decide that they are probably not going home, develop a network of friends here, and find financial stability. A few become transnational—living here, but building a future in their home country. Most, however, decide that the U.S. is their home. This is what happened to me.

I came to California from my native Puerto Rico when I was twenty-one. I moved here to finish my education. I was lucky enough to go to a good college in Puerto Rico and came to California to obtain a master's degree. Having been born an American citizen, I never thought of myself as an immigrant. I grew up with strong Latino values, but appreciated American ones also. Puerto Rico's calendar included indigenous holidays as well as American holidays, and we celebrated both with pride.

I never thought I was different from other Americans, but when I arrived here, I soon realized I was. My new American friends thought of me as a foreigner, and I had to constantly explain that Puerto Rico is a commonwealth of the U. S.. My new Latino immigrant friends also thought of me as "different." Unlike many of them, I could return home at any time, did not have to work two jobs to pay my bills, was fluent in Spanish and English, and was educated and confident.

> "It may help you to know that a vast number of immigrants reach the acceptance stage."

Still, like most immigrants, I felt terribly alone, isolated, and homesick. I missed my family, especially on Sundays. Life was not as exciting in California. It took me years to adjust to my new home.

I was very good at denying my own pain. When I would talk to my family on Sundays, my dad would ask, "How are you, mi'ja?" I would always say, "I am fine, Papi; I love it here." Deep inside, I felt sad and nostalgic. Because moving here was my own decision, I felt I had to hide my true feelings. I had to pretend that everything was fine when, actually, I wanted to go back home. Wasn't going back an admission of failure? The thought of disappointing my parents and myself made me even more determined to stay and succeed.

There were times, though, that I was happy here. For example, when I babysat for an American family who treated me like one of them. They were a family of three children, a mother, and a father. Strict and loving, their values were similar to the ones I grew up with. Having dinner with them reminded me of my family lunches. At the same time, I felt I was betraying my family. "Maybe I do belong here, and I really don't miss it back home," I told myself. Then I would feel confused and cry.

Two years after I graduated from my master's program, I applied to five or six public relations agencies in the area. I had been working at a non-profit organization, in charge of the Hispanic department, but I wanted to work at a PR agency where I could be exposed to both the English language media and the Latino media. Bilingual and bicultural, I could read, write, and speak Spanish, English, and French. Wouldn't I be an asset to any company? It seemed so to me, yet I was turned down by most of the agencies I applied to.

Those that were initially interested in hiring me were involved in very few projects directed to the Latino market. At the time, less than a handful

> "I realized that I am neither from here, nor from there; I belong to both worlds."

of PR firms dealt with the Latino market and even fewer were Latino-owned. I was told I needed more experience writing in English, which made me angry. Hadn't I just gone to school for six years and worked for two to prove that I was as good as the next person? Resentment was ever-present. I began looking for a job in the Latino market. "I am Puerto Rican and Spanish is my first language," I kept repeating. But the jobs would go to other Latinos who were born here. I applied for a job in the general market. "I am bicultural and educated. I can do any task," I would reason. But the jobs would go to other candidates with more experience. How could I get more experience if no one was willing to give me a chance?

One of my first jobs was at a large PR firm, one of the initial agencies to have a Hispanic division. I had to deal with a Latina who was born and raised here, and was not fluent in Spanish. Of course, I spoke Spanish fluently and could write in both languages. She didn't like that—after I was hired, she managed to make my job difficult and to impress upon the fact that I was not knowledgeable enough about the Latino market in California, and thus convinced the employer that I was not suitable for the job. I realized then, that regardless of our cultural similarities, my qualifications posed a threat to other Latinas. I resented that they resented me! It took a few years before I met Latinas who liked me for the person I was and didn't judge me for my background. Those women were welcoming and supportive, and they are still my friends today.

It wasn't until I'd been here for fifteen years, that I felt California was "home." Much has changed since my arrival to attend college here. Today my education and my heritage are valued by American companies that want to explore the Hispanic market, as well as by Latino-owned companies. After I left the public relations arena, I became a freelance writer for *La Opinión*. My parenting column ran in the paper once a week for eleven years, making me the first Latina immigrant to write specifically to Latino parents raising children in this country. I raised my children with a value system that included both Latino and American ways. In my quest to find that balance, I realized that I am neither from here, nor from there; I belong to both worlds.

Moving Through the Stages of Immigrant Adjustment

Whether it takes months or years, most Latinos eventually adjust to their new life in America. We may think it will never happen, and then one day we find ourselves saying, "I honestly feel I belong here. My children and I are fitting into this culture, just like everyone else."

Coming to a new country is not an easy task. Some individuals take longer to adjust than others. We may find ourselves stuck in one particular stage due to our personal circumstances. Maybe finding a job or overcoming the language barrier is harder than we thought. Perhaps our husband, our neighbor, our coworker, or our child is adjusting faster than we are, and we may resent them for that. It is important to understand that we go through these stages at our own pace and that other immigrants are also struggling to adjust.

Today's cultural differences are somewhat minimized due to globalization and the Internet, and as a result, the process of adjustment can be easier. Values are understood differently in each country, and it is up to us—no matter where we come from—to stay open and receptive to the new, while finding ways to preserve the old.

Whether we clean houses, work in a factory, travel into space, or deliver the news on television every night, as immigrants, we all have a hard time adjusting to this country. But we ALL can succeed—as individuals and as parents.

Success Story: Jorge Ramos

Every night for the last twenty-five years, Jorge Ramos has delivered the news to millions of Latinos across the United States and Puerto Rico. His story is that of a young man who emigrated in search of the American dream. It took time, determination, and adjustments, but his dream eventually came true.

"I came to the United States when I was twenty-five years old. I came alone and didn't know anyone. I remember vividly that I carried a guitar, a suitcase, and a briefcase. It was the night of January 2, 1983. I can still remember the feeling of freedom. With the $2,000 I got from selling my car and some other savings, I decided to come to Los Angeles. I was aware that I had made a very important decision in my life.

"Mexico City in the '80s suffocated me. It was after a censorship incident with a television station that I decided to try my luck in the

United States as an independent journalist. But my first job was as a waiter and a cashier. My initial excitement faded. I began feeling sad and homesick. Calling home was expensive, and I didn't want my family to know about my feelings or think I was not happy about moving to America. I also missed the food—boy, did I miss it! Most of my conversations would begin with, 'Back home,' without realizing that comparisons were not really appreciated by most people around me. For years, I would figure the exchange rate between dollars and Mexican pesos when going to a store. In other words, I was living in the United States, but mentally, I was still in Mexico.

"Having an accent did not help either, especially when trying to communicate at a bank or on the telephone. My name was difficult to pronounce in English, so I changed it to George to make it easier. Years later, I understood that an accent and a name tell a story and speak of a person's origin. I remember the time my news director invited me for Thanksgiving. I had no idea what Thanksgiving was! Sometimes, I was not sure where I belonged, Mexico or the United States. Getting my green card gave me a feeling of belonging to the United States while also allowing me to travel to Mexico and feel less homesick. It was hard for me to adjust, but I was determined to make it happen. I wanted to succeed in this country. Once I found my first job as a reporter in the local Univision station, things began to fall into place. I realized that the United States could really become my adoptive country.

"Today, I feel that I am part of both countries. I can relate to the Chilean author Isabel Allende who said that after the terrorists' attacks of September 11, 2001, she feels that she is as American as she is Chilean. I feel the same way; I am from Mexico and from the United States. My future is here. My two children were born in the United States. They speak Spanish and English, and I am about to celebrate over twenty-five years in this country. This is a land of opportunities, and I am living proof of the American dream. I don't have any plans to go anywhere else."

Tips for Latino Immigrants as They Move Towards Adjusting

Adjusting to a new life is not easy. There are physical, personal, and psychological struggles. It takes time and determination. But it can happen. Here are tips to help you get through all stages of immigrant adjustment.

1.   By immigrating, you have made an important decision to better your life. This was and is your goal. No matter what you are feeling or what difficulties you are facing, try to make the best of it and remember the long-term benefits.

2.   Know that changes are difficult—even good changes. Try not to resist the changes that are happening to you, but welcome them. At the end of the journey, when you are successfully balancing two cultures, you will be glad for the experience of change. It will enrich your life in many ways.

3.   Remember that you are not alone in this process, even though it may feel like it at times. Seek out fellow immigrants at church, or your local library or community center. Share your feelings and concerns, and you will probably find other people who are experiencing the same things you are.

4.   Try to stay positive, and remember that one day, you will be a source of inspiration to new immigrant parents.

5.   Every person assimilates sooner or later, and everyone does so at his or her own pace. Respect your own pace and avoid comparisons. If it takes you longer than your friends and family to move through a stage, accept that and be patient.

6.   It is important that you speak English fluently. You will feel more confident, and it will help you adjust. Chapter 2 deals directly with the challenges of learning English and offers many resources to help you on this path.

7.   Remember that you are an individual first before you are a parent. You must adjust to your new country before you can

help your kids adjust. Give yourself the time and resources you need to succeed.

My Parenting Journal

We all made the choice to come to America and must adjust to our new life here. Writing down our feelings might help us to understand and accept the changes we're going through. On the blank page, write down the thoughts and feelings that come to your mind while reading this chapter. You may also want to answer the following questions to get started.

1. Which stage of adjustment do you believe you are experiencing right now?
2. Have you found any kind of balance between your two cultures?
3. If you have not found balance yet, why not? What might be holding you back?
4. Have you accepted the fact that your life is changing because you're part of a new country? Are you embracing the changes or fighting them?
5. Do you see your life in America in a positive way, or do you keep criticizing the way things are here?
6. If you are feeling negative, see if you can find one thing each week to praise about your life here—even if it's something very small. Having this kind of gratitude can create more positive feelings.
7. What kind of help might you need to keep moving forward in your adjustment?
8. What are your ideas for where you can seek help if you need it?
9. Do you know of any role models you can use for inspiration as you strive towards balance? It always helps to have people to look up to who have accomplished the goals you have set for yourself. Even if those role models are celebrities you will never meet in person, just knowing about them can help.

Chapter 2: Latino Children Bicultural Blues

"It's hard for me to make friends. Most of the kids in my school have been together for a long time. Sometimes, my new friends don't understand my parents' ways, and my parents don't understand how hard it is for me to blend in."
—*Julia, age 14*

Whether an immigrant child arrives in this country at five, ten, or fifteen years of age, she or he will most likely react in ways that can be extremely challenging for parents. Everything a child knew about how to get along in the world is drastically transformed by this relocation. Even if he is around family and other immigrant kids, he may still feel isolated, different, uncomfortable, and lost.

How do immigrant children react to being the outsider in a new environment? Some of them act up or misbehave. Others may gravitate to friends who make them feel like they belong, whether they are Latino or not. Americanized kids may influence a new immigrant to change his behavior, dress differently, and even treat his parents differently. Such changes might include refusing to speak Spanish at home, ignoring a parent's authority, or falling behind in school.

"Even if your time is limited, your children and teenagers need your attention."

Latino kids who are still struggling to be accepted, or are rebelling against their new environment may influence a newcomer to rebel along with them. Antisocial behavior at school, going against parental rules, and even breaking the law can be ways that a young immigrant acts out his discomfort and frustration. Some children get involved with gangs, others might shun friendships and withdraw from other kids altogether. The lucky ones have parents, stepparents, grandparents, or other mentors to help them during this transition.

While parents have to cope with their own troubles, it is their responsibility to help their children cope also. Sometimes, immigrant parents are so busy trying to make ends meet that they may inadvertently ignore what's going on with their kids. Even if your time is limited, your children and teenagers need your attention. They need you to be there for them, to ask them about their friends and their school, to discipline them and make sure they do their homework, and to be interested in their future. Even though you may think you have no influence, that your son's or daughter's friends count for more than you do, no one is more important in your child's life than you are. The example you set, and your time, guidance, and love, are priceless.

Preparing for the Move

Mary Klem, a marriage and family therapist, believes that the process of assimilating into a new culture is difficult for both adults and children: "First off, how does one leave everything behind, start over, work full time, raise kids, and also find time to learn a new language and culture? From a child's standpoint, the process of bridging two cultures can be stressful. Parents need to be conscientious of their children's stress levels."

How well children adjust to their new environment depends on their parents. Do the parents want their children to become integrated into the new culture—or not? How well do immigrant parents prepare their children ahead of time? Is assimilation the goal? If so, how do parents achieve that, given the circumstances? What if the family is moving together at the same time and the parents don't really know what to expect?

According to Klem, it is important for parents to address this issue with their children initially, when the family first makes the decision to move to the States. Parents should explain to children, to the best of their abilities, what their new home will be like. Furthermore, parents should express to children that they may experience some really great things about the new culture, but may also experience some things that may seem very different or odd to them. Let the children know this is normal and that their parents will help them all along the way.

Our children are often conflicted about the differences between their home life and their school and social lives. They may complain about our decisions and insist that we change our standards to more closely resemble the way their friends' parents handle things. "It is a fact that children want to belong," said psychologist Ana Nogales. "If they feel rejected by the new environment, then it is difficult to make the adjustment. Especially if they are seen like 'the other culture.' This is why some immigrant children feel more comfortable with other immigrant children because this gives them a sense of belonging. On the other hand, once children—and adults—are exposed to a multicultural environment and allow themselves to become more accepting, it eventually becomes easier to relate to it."

Parents are their children's facilitators in adjusting to the new culture. Even in the same family, siblings won't necessarily adjust in the same way or at the same rate. One's personality, age, and confidence level—as well as the parent's emotional support of that child—play a role. The extended family also plays a role.

> "Talk to your children and tell them the truth about what their life will be like in the States before they arrive."

If there is little available support from extended family—including aunts, uncles, cousins, and grandparents—parents may tend to become more protective, less flexible, and less trusting of their new environment. They might worry that in the quest to belong, their kids will get involved with the wrong crowd.

Economic concerns can also affect how a parent deals with a child's integration into a new culture. Like the experts, I believe that parents need to be honest with their children and discuss with them the pros and cons of living here before they arrive. They should talk to the children about what their daily lives will be like and the possibilities that there won't be a lot of time to spend together as a family, but that mom and dad will do their best. It is important to share that mom and dad might not be able to help with homework because they might not understand the language. They need to share that they might be living with a family member for a while because the cost of living in America is expensive and they will have to wait before moving to their own place. Older children also need to be prepared for the possibility that although there are no federal or state laws that prohibit undocumented students from attending college, some factors may make this difficult. Admission policies may vary, depending on the institution, and paying for school might be difficult because their status makes them ineligible to apply for federal financial aid. That being said, reassure children that mom and dad will do everything they can to help them achieve a higher education by seeking advice and direction from teachers or other parents.

Immigrant parents are often so preoccupied with their financial situation that they might tend to sideline the emotional status of their children. This can leave the kids with few tools to handle right from wrong, such as when confronted by violence, drugs, pregnancy, and gangs. It is important for parents to keep the lines of communication open to discuss all of these issues and provide as much guidance as possible during their kids' transition, even if they need to ask for help from other parents, relatives, or teachers. The more we surround our children with people who can offer a listening ear, a piece of advice, a shoulder to cry on at the right time or a positive role model, the more tools our children will have to handle a major situation and the more comfortable they will be to share it.

When Parents Move First

What about when parents immigrate to the States first, leaving their children behind with other relatives? The adjustment is difficult for those children that are left behind. Parents are not there on a daily basis, and they try to monitor their children's well-being via telephone calls, with the disciplinary reins given to grandparents or other relatives. This situation is hard for the child. He may feel alone, neglected, frustrated, and sad. His parents want control of his life, but they are far away. The family union has been disrupted. When the child joins the parents, he often leaves behind a more rural environment with different cultural and social characteristics than the ones he will find in his new environment. Because parents are working so hard to make it in their new home, children might find themselves having less time with their parents. Everything is an adjustment: school, language, friends, and food, just to name a few. "Again, parents need to remain watchful over children's stress levels. Talk to them about their stressors. Ask them about and talk about any social or academic issues that may pop up. Have discussions about their observations on their new life. Validating children's concerns and listening to them is essential. Open dialogue between parents and children, even about difficult issues, sets parents and kids up for a strong and positive relationship," said Klem.

Most immigrant children come here with the illusion of reuniting with the parents they knew before the parents emigrated, the parents they had back home. They quickly discover that the parents have changed; there is a different way of life here, maybe a new spouse or partner, new children born here, and demanding jobs. Jealousies, reproaches, and hostilities can result. "Children often come to this country with no previous emotional preparation, and when they meet the new version of their family, they may be resentful," said Klem.

It is important to maintain an open dialogue about why parents moved and what life will be like in the new country. It is paramount for parents to share their own experiences of when they first came, so that children understand it is okay to feel insecure and different, and are reminded that all those feelings are temporary, and that they will make friends and adjust to their new life soon enough, just like their parents did.

Listening to the Children

The following are four stories from young immigrants whose parents and grandparents helped them adapt to American life, while still holding on to their Latino values. As you read about how these families dealt with the challenge of Americanization, perhaps you'll discover similarities to your child's difficulties, and learn valuable new ways to deal with them.

Marlon's Story: It Takes a Village to Assimilate

Marlon was three years old when his mother, Susana, moved to the States, leaving him and his two older brothers in Guatemala with their maternal grandmother. She came looking for work opportunities, which, at the time, were not available in her country. When Marlon was four years old, his grandmother died, so he and his siblings went to live with their aunt's family. "Life at my aunt's was difficult," Marlon said. "She really didn't have time to parent us or teach us anything. We followed the house rules, but there was no emphasis on learning." Marlon's birth father had abandoned the family when Marlon was only a year old, so the only father figure Marlon and his brothers had was the man his mother married when she came to the U.S. His name was Frank, and he was half Mexican-American and half Canadian. Frank and Susana visited Marlon and his brothers in Guatemala when Marlon was five. "That was really the first memory I have of my parents, and even though Frank was my stepfather, we really connected as father and son," Marlon said. During that visit, Frank became the father the boys never had.

It would be another eight to nine years before Marlon would see his mother and stepfather again. At fourteen, he moved to the States. By then, his mother had gone to school, learned the language, and adapted to American norms. Marlon believes his adjustment to life in the States was much easier than his mother's, primarily because he had attended a private Catholic school in Guatemala where the curriculum included a course in English. "By the time I got here, my mother already spoke the language, and my father and my grandmother spoke English fluently. That helped me with the adjustment, but I still wasn't fluent in English." Because of his mother's work and her move to this country when Marlon was growing up, they don't have the best relationship, but he believes his mother loves him unconditionally. His mother has not been involved in his education, but she supports his drive. She is a very loving and nurturing person and has taught Marlon about being kind and caring to others. "She is not the kind of mom I would go to when I feel down or when I need to talk, but she tries hard to make up for all the years she wasn't there," he said.

Marlon didn't speak very good English when he first arrived, so he couldn't communicate with any of his teachers fluently. He initially asked a friend to translate for him, but he still felt uncomfortable and lonely in high school. The social customs of his fellow students were vastly different than what Marlon had known in Guatemala, leaving him feeling terribly out of place. One of the first things he noticed was how his American friends treated their parents and teachers. "The kids showed no respect for their elders; they didn't want to follow the rules. Back home, I would have been spanked if I misspoke to an elder!" he said.

His step-grandmother, Isabel, took on the job of helping him adapt to his new life. Though born in Texas and raised in California, Isabel's parents were of Mexican descent. "She came from a very traditional Latino background," Marlon said, "and applied that to her parenting. She was strict!" Isabel made Marlon read English books for two hours every day. His stepfather spoke English all the time and helped Marlon with his schoolwork. "He guided me and lectured me about life in the U.S.. He would talk to me about the danger of drugs, about behavior, and social awareness. He was a good mentor and a respectable father to me," Marlon said.

For Marlon, the first two years in the States were definitely the most challenging: "Because of my language barriers, I had to repeat eighth grade and my middle school experience was hard. I felt like I had to make myself look dignified, strong, and approachable. I guess my maturity attracted the younger students. They looked up to me, which made me a role model to them. In high school, things changed for the better. There, no one knew me as part of the 'in' crowd, but more as a student who was always curious about everything and hung out in the teachers' classrooms acquiring knowledge. I showed interest and effort and the teachers appreciated that."

Despite the struggles as a teenager, Marlon is now happy and well-adjusted to living with two cultures. Today, he is in graduate school studying public policy and administration. He plans to attain a doctoral degree in education policy or leadership, and a Ph.D. in public administration.

Araceli's Story: Overcoming the Stigma of Being Undocumented

Araceli's parents immigrated to the States a few years before she was born. Finding the adjustment too difficult, they returned to Mexico. They came back—this time with eighteen-month-old Araceli—when they realized they had a better life in this country and had to give it another try. Now nineteen, Araceli is amazed at how difficult it was for her parents to bring her here. Not only did they risk crossing the border, but they also left two other daughters behind, an infant and a four year old. Once here, they tried getting jobs in many places, but their inability to speak or understand English made it impossible. Without a job, or with only one of them working, it was hard making ends meet. "My mother had to do some real good money management so that we could live semi-decently," said Araceli.

Childcare was also difficult. Araceli's aunt took care of ten kids, including Araceli and her sisters, so that all of the immigrant adults were able to work and make money. "My aunt did her part in feeding us and keeping us in her backyard, but we took care of basically everything else amongst ourselves," Araceli said.

After twenty years here, Araceli's parents still do not speak English fluently, but they have embraced some American customs such as celebrating Thanksgiving and hosting Fourth of July family gatherings. They have learned to be more liberal. For example, in Mexico, parents are really strict about letting their children go out, especially girls, but in America, immigrant parents tend to become more trusting of letting their children go out without supervision.

"In some ways, adjusting has been harder for me. Growing up, I was afraid to tell people that I wasn't born here, that I lived in a garage with a family of six, and that at one point, speaking in English made me self-conscious. My parents had bigger problems, like keeping a roof above our heads," Araceli said.

Araceli has mixed feelings about her immigrant status. During her sophomore year in high school, everyone talked about getting a driver's license. "Everyone came running to me full of excitement and said, 'Hey Cheli, are you going to get your license, too?' The first thought in my head was, 'No, I can't, I wasn't born here!!' but what came out my mouth was, 'No, my parents can't afford it right now. I'll just wait until I turn eighteen.' There was always a time when I had to lie," she said.

Araceli's parents are undocumented, which has resulted in practical, economic, and social problems. "My parents never sat me down and told me I was different from American children," Araceli said. "It wasn't until I got older that I saw the differences between an American teenager and an undocumented teenager. It was hard to see my American friends do things I couldn't do, like drive a car, or go away to college in another state or abroad.

Over the years, Araceli's parents adapted to more American habits. Still, Araceli struggled with the fact that her papers were pending for a while. "Knowing that I was

"My faith has helped me understand that sometimes, things happen to make us work harder."

not born here, and going to college, I was affected a lot more than when I was in high school. One would think that financial aid is based on merit, but that is not true; it is all based on where one is born. I couldn't apply to the colleges that I preferred to attend, because I wouldn't be able to get financial aid. But these injustices have taught me to be compassionate, accepting, and more tolerant of others. My faith has helped me understand that sometimes, things happen to make us work harder. I have become a stronger person and it has helped me accomplish my goals and dreams," she said.

Araceli credits her mother and her sister, Maria, for helping her through the difficult times in her young immigrant life: "My mother taught me the benefits of being bilingual. She is not fluent herself, but she understands that if one speaks both languages, one has better job opportunities. My sister pushed me in every way to apply to college, to meet all the deadlines, to do better, be better, and to want better. I am grateful for that. She and my mother have been the best examples of strong Latina women in my life."

These two women have influenced her more than her friends. "I have adjusted well in the American system, but not to the point where my friends have a greater influence than my parents. I admit that there have been times when I've complained to my parents because I wanted to do things my friends were doing, but now that I am older, I understand their ways better," she said.

Araceli graduated with a bachelor's degree in psychology and a minor in human services. Currently she works for a private, non-profit mental health agency as a therapeutic behavior specialist. She is now a U.S. citizen and looks forward to voting for the second time in the upcoming presidential elections.

In her view, raising children with an appreciation and respect for both sides of their cultural background is a great benefit. "One beautiful thing about being born in a different country is being able to relate to both cultures. I am able to communicate in both languages, Spanish and English, and I can relate to more people than someone who only speaks one language. It opens many doors that wouldn't be available if it wasn't for my background and where I come from. Understanding two different cultures allows me to appreciate the different types of beauty that people have individually, regardless of their economic status," she said.

Carlitos' Story: Staying Out of Trouble and Finding a Cultural Balance

The oldest of four children, Carlitos came to America when he was ten. He and his brother, along with their father, worked as street merchants to help support the family. They have been arrested and fined for selling on the street. He also recalls a time when he was arrested by a police officer for no reason: "I was doing nothing wrong; he just didn't like the way I looked." Because they are undocumented immigrants and don't speak English, Carlitos's parents work at jobs that pay only minimum wage.

"I don't have the same opportunities as other kids my age," he said. "Other kids have more time to study and keep up with their homework. They have time to look into ways that can help them further their education, like scholarships, and they have time to do fun things with family and friends. My family and I, we just barely make it through the day."

His frustration led Carlitos to join a gang for a while, until tragedy struck—his best friend, Ramón, was killed. Carlitos and Ramón had been friends since fifth grade when Carlitos first came to America. "Ramón came over and introduced himself, and from then on we were friends until he died. He offered me help and support when I needed it most, and I will never forget him. But Ramón chose a different path. I realized when he died that that was not the life I wanted. I decided to stay in high school. Even if it was a struggle, I was going to achieve an education," he said.

His parents supported his decision and encouraged him to continue his education. "Even when I was hanging with the wrong crowd, my parents never abandoned me. They always told me that a good education is the greatest gift they can give me and my siblings, and that no one can take that away from me. From them, I have learned the value of hard work and dedication to family, and how important it is to give back to others," he said. At times, Carlitos's parents worry that his American friends have more influence than they do, but he assures them that no one would ever impact his life more.

Today, Carlitos enjoys going to college, and tutors younger kids to help them adjust to the new culture. "My parents helped me by making me go to school when I just wanted to drop out. They taught me that life includes good and bad experiences, and about right versus wrong. Isn't that what every parent should do in any culture? I am determined to make a difference. I made a promise to myself and to my family that nothing would stop me from pursuing an education and a career," he said. Carlitos is on his way to achieving his goals!

María's Story: Overcoming Two Cultures with Gratitude

Born in Southern California, Maria is a first generation Mexican-American. Her parents are both Mexicans from Central Mexico. Her mom emigrated to the United States at fourteen years of age and her dad at sixteen. Maria's mom was fifteen and her father was nineteen when Maria was born. For the first six years of her life, Maria was raised speaking only Spanish and was exposed to English only when she entered school. At school, the majority of students were Spanish speakers, which made learning English very difficult. She then went to Mexico to live with her grandmother, and forgot most of her English, even though she took private classes some of the time there to ensure she wouldn't lose it completely.

For Maria, being Mexican-American is a unique experience and one she wouldn't change. Although it has presented some challenges along the way, Maria believes that overcoming those difficult times has provided her with strength, an essential factor in being successful in every undertaking. However, at times, her bicultural experience has proved confusing and frustrating: "I feel that I missed out on 'American-only' experiences, like music, traditions, idiomatic phrases, to name a few, which somehow prevents me from fully enjoying or fully engaging in American-only experiences. Similarly, because I wasn't born and entirely raised in Mexico, I also sometimes feel that I missed out on 'Mexican-only' experiences. Such sentiments have made me feel like an outsider at times. Undoubtedly, however, I can say that being exposed to two different cultures gives one the opportunity to pick and choose the best values, experiences, and traditions from both worlds."

One of the things that Maria appreciates most about being bicultural is what the cultural subtleties can reveal about the people who speak that language. "That is fascinating," she said. "When communicating with other bilinguals, one doesn't have to explain cultural subtleties." Biculturalism has taught her to be open, to judge a different culture without prejudice. "Being bicultural doesn't mean behaving fifty percent this way and fifty percent the 'other' way. Balance doesn't mean an equal amount all the time. Sometimes, one culture is more present than the other. Always, the presence of culture is possible via languages. In familiar places, Spanish feels most safe and comfortable. With family, I speak mostly Spanish. At work, with colleagues, English is spoken. With my students, I speak mostly Spanish. With some friends, I speak English, and Spanish with others, and then there are some with whom I can switch between English and Spanish! Being myself is what keeps me balanced between both languages and both cultures."

Maria and her husband, who is of mixed Scottish, German, and Mexican descent, have a two-year-old son. When I asked her about similarities in which she and her son were raised, she said that her son is being raised with the same religion she was. Teaching her son Spanish is a similarity, as is teaching him the values that are important to her Latino culture: her religion, the value of family and customs, how to respect the elders and, being bilingual, among others. In terms of differences, it is important to her that her son learns independence at an early age: "In my opinion, this is a valuable skill that will help him become a better person in this world. Equally important, is to teach him how to be assertive. Children can teach us so much if we only listen to them."

Like many other Latino parents today, Maria disciplines her son by being consistent in the application of house rules and by modeling good behavior. She doesn't believe in spanking, unlike earlier generations of Latino parents: "I think my way of discipline is more effective. I'm lucky I have been exposed to alternative ways of disciplining children. I'm not sure that my grandmother and mother were ever exposed to alternative parenting methods themselves. They did their best." Maria is very proud of her grandmother and her mother: "My grandmother and mother raised me and taught me values that I hope to teach my son. They taught me the importance of having a good work ethic, self-respect, and assertiveness."

Maria is raising her son bilingual and bicultural. The language part is sometimes a challenge. "At preschool, he mostly hears English. At home, he mixes the languages. He knows some words in Spanish and others in English. For example, he will say 'apple' and I repeat '*manzana*.' He'll say, 'No, apple,' thinking that I am saying a different word rather than simply in a different language. At this age, he doesn't quite understand that there is more than one way of referring to the same thing. That's a challenge. He might be too young to understand one language over the other one. Another challenge is speaking to him in Spanish in public. For some reason, I feel that people will judge me if I speak to him in Spanish in front of them. Will they think that I don't think learning English is important? This is curious to me. I don't quite understand why I feel this way," she said.

Maria's hope is that her son learns to appreciate both languages, both cultures, and beyond: "I don't want him to feel that one language is more important than the other—just different, depending on the situation."

Maria believes that being exposed to more than one culture is an opportunity to enrich children's lives. Most children in the world don't have this opportunity. Children will respect and value being bilingual and bicultural only if they believe their parents show and demonstrate respect for their own cultures, their own languages, and for others.

Today, Maria is a professor of Spanish and the Modern Language Coordinator at Napa Valley College in Northern California, and the founder of *Spanish Language Consulting*, a firm that offers language services: translating, editing, proofreading, and training. She is the Spanish language consultant to the NBC Universal show, *Nina's World*, available on Sprout Network. "As a bicultural person," she said, "I feel that I represent the best of both worlds. *¡Sí se puede!*"

Tips for Latino Parents to Help with Their Children's Adjustment

When our kids start behaving in ways that anger or bewilder us, we might feel that we have failed them. Though we may feel that our children's Americanized friends have more influence than we do, as parents, we will always have more influence if we aren't afraid to use it. To help you balance American values and Latino values, I offer the following suggestions. These ideas can help both you and your children better accept the new way of life here and find a compromise that you can both live with. There are also many tips and ideas in Chapters 5 and 6.

1. Try not to be angry if your children are acting out. Your children are going through a difficult period. They are trying to adjust to a new life. As parents, you need to help them do that.
2. Make time for your children. If both you and your spouse work outside the home, have dinner together every night, or as often as possible. If you and your spouse work nightshifts, spend time together as a family on the weekends. Go to the park or the beach, or cook dinner together at home. Do whatever it is that you would do as a family back in your native country.
3. Get to know your children's friends. Invite them over, even if they come from a different background than yours, or don't speak the same language. If there is a friend you don't like or you think is a bad influence in your child's life, talk to your child about it. Give him a chance to explain what it is about that friend that attracts him. Be open to the possibility of changing your mind.
4. Invite the parents of your children's friends over for dinner. The more you make an effort to be part of your children's lives, the more valued they will feel. Plus, if your children know

you may invite people over to your home, they may think twice before befriending someone you might disapprove of.

5. Trust your children. If they grow up knowing right from wrong, it doesn't matter where they are, they will follow the rules.

6. Be involved in their lives. Perhaps the only difference between a boy who joins a gang and a boy who doesn't, is that the boy who doesn't has parents who are very present in his life.

7. Expect the best; be the best. Trust yourself.

My Parenting Journal

Immigrant parents and children need to be prepared for the changes they'll go through and keep the lines of communication open. Use this chapter to open up a dialogue with your kids. Talk about their feelings about being here and about having left their prior life behind. Share your feelings. Here are some questions to get you started.

1. Are you happy here in America? If not, what exactly is bothering you? How might you change that? The best way to ensure that your kids are happy, is for you to be happy yourself.

2. How are your children adjusting to their new country and their new lifestyle? What seems to be going well? What seems to be a struggle?

3. If your children are struggling, do you know what specifically is bothering them?

4. If you don't know, how can you find out? Would asking them work? What about talking to other parents, teachers, or the school principal?

5. What can you do to help change your child's experience of America? Make a list of everything you can think of, including spending more time together, seeking out role models, or asking a friend, relative, or church member for guidance.

6. Are you making enough time for the family? If not, why not? What changes could you make to ensure more family time together? Even a small amount of time is better than none.

7. Have you met your children's friends? Their parents? If not, why not?

8. What can you do to make sure you get a chance to meet your children's friends and their parents? You might want to start by simply going up to the door when you drop your child off at a friend's house and saying hello. Even if hello is all you can say, it's a start.

9. Do you make an effort to meet your children's teachers? What might you do to make sure you have a meeting with them soon? If you are worried about your ability to communicate, see if you can ask someone who speaks both English and your native language to join you in the meeting.

Chapter 3: Balancing Two Cultures

"For twenty years, I have been in this country. My two kids were born here. I was scared that they wouldn't appreciate their heritage. But I was determined. They grew up with the two cultures. I adjusted to the new one and helped them appreciate mine. Today they are both happy and proud that they are half Latino and half American."
—Teresa, age 45

"I was the first one in my family to go to college. My parents were very involved in my education from the moment we moved here. It was important for them that I had everything they didn't have. It was hard for them to accept so many things...but we made it. It can be done."
—Lupita, age 24

Whether we brought our children to this country, or gave birth to them here, they grew up with two sets of values that are very often at odds. Successful parenting means balancing what our two cultures have to offer, or achieving cultural integration. In other words, successful parenting means adapting to the positive aspects of American culture, while at the same time encouraging your child's sense of Latino pride. It is up to us to help our kids accept their bicultural identity and reach a balance that honors the best of both worlds. So, the next time your eight-year-old comes home and announces he is not speaking Spanish anymore, sit down with him and explain to him the advantages of being bilingual. Remind him of how much smarter he is because he speaks two languages instead of just one.

> "Successful parenting means adapting to the positive aspects of American culture, while at the same time encouraging your child's sense of Latino pride."

When your fourteen-year-old complains that she hates her new school, ask her why she feels this way. She might share with you how difficult it is for her to make new friends. You might want to call her teacher or school counselor and arrange for a meeting. Even if you don't speak English well, you could find a friend to go with you to translate. It's likely that the teacher or counselor will have resources your daughter could benefit from, as well as advice on how she might make friends more easily. However you choose to deal with the situation, it is important for your daughter to know that you are willing to listen to her, that you care about what she's going through, and that you want to help her.

The same goes for your ten-year-old son who gets in trouble at school. His school might ask you to come in because your son has been in a fight. When you get there, his teacher may explain that he is acting up in class, along with a group of friends he's fallen in with. She might tell you that this kind of thing often happens with children who emigrate from another country and feel anxious about being at a new school in a new country. Children often try to gain acceptance by going along with the crowd—in this case, the wrong one. As parents, you need to sit down with your child and ask him what he is feeling. He needs to know that you understand how hard it is for him to be in a new place and that you want to help him. Tell him that you love him and that you know it is hard for him to have to adjust to a new country, far away from everything he loves. Tell him that life is going to get better here and that he needs to give it a chance and choose the right path. Let him know that you are watching out for him and that you want the best for him. Your encouragement and support will make a difference.

Celebrate Your Native Culture with Your Children

The best way to teach our children to love and appreciate our native culture is to live by example. It is up to parents to look for ways that will expose children to their Latino heritage, wherever they live. By celebrating our customs and traditions at home, we teach our children to embrace them. These traditions become part of their daily lives and it is something they expect.

Martha, a first generation Mexican-American, teaches her kids about her culture through food and professional gatherings: "My kids and I eat tamales at Christmastime, traditional foods during major holidays, and certain dishes all year round. I always tell them about their *abuelitos* and what their life was like in Mexico and in the U.S. in keeping our culture as part of our daily lives. They are growing up knowing how proud I am to be a Latina, how blessed they are to be Latinos, and feel that pride. It is my gift to them."

Patty, a Colombian immigrant, came to this country when she was sixteen: "People would laugh when I spoke English because of my strong accent. It has been different for my children. They were born here and they speak both languages. Maintaining my roots became more important when I had them." To that end, Patty often cooks Colombian food, and the family visits Colombia every year. They read Spanish books whenever they can, and she took her girls to live in Spain for a year to improve their Spanish.

Magali moved from Peru to the United States where she met her husband, Jorge, who is Argentine. "When I had children, I wanted to make sure they spoke Spanish, so I would read to them in Spanish at home all the time. When both girls entered preschool, they spoke no English and it was a difficult period for them because they couldn't communicate easily. I do believe that this experience made them a little resentful towards speaking Spanish because they refused to speak it for a while to avoid being embarrassed. However, that changed when they were around eleven or twelve, once they realized that being Hispanic was cool and speaking another language had a huge advantage in this country. Traveling back to our countries of origin and being able to communicate with family and friends in Spanish made them appreciate the benefits of being bilingual. The girls were brought up celebrating their Hispanic traditions while living in this country and they love it," Magali said.

As for me, my children grew up with Puerto Rican food as part of their weekly menu: *arroz con maiz* (rice with corn), *arroz con pollo* (rice with chicken), and *arroz con garbanzos y chorizos* (rice with garbanzo beans and Spanish sausage). Spanish is spoken often, but not as regularly as I would like. In an effort to include my husband, who doesn't speak Spanish in our daily conversations, I stopped speaking Spanish to the children as they got older. They now speak very little Spanish, except for when they are in Puerto Rico, visiting my family. My son has a love for his ethnicity—half Latino, half Greek—and he is very proud to announce it to everyone he meets. I love that he looks forward to visiting the island and that he enjoys knowing all about my life there and my culture. My daughter likes to tell her friends about my cooking and about the Latino culture in which I grew up. When anticipating her trip to Spain during her senior year of college, she was most excited to be living with a family that would speak Spanish to her all the time!

Blending the Best of the Two Cultures

When my children were little, two or three years old, they went from speaking English with their dad to speaking Spanish with me. I was in awe of how they transitioned from one language to the next within seconds; it was automatic. As immigrant parents, that effortlessness is what we should strive for in our children. It is up to us to teach them to love their past, their native culture, and appreciate their present, their new culture, and embrace their future, the blending of both. The following are five stories about families who found ways to successfully blend their two cultures.

Margarita's Story: My U.S. Education, My Career, and My Love of the Mexican Culture Inspires My Daughters

Margarita was fourteen years old when she came to the U.S from Mexico "I was alone when I came and that was scary," she said, "but I took it as challenge. It was always important to me to preserve my Mexican culture, but it was difficult when I was surrounded by such a multicultural environment." Perhaps because she knew that she wanted to improve her life, it was somewhat easier for Margarita to open herself to her new culture: "I found the balance because I wanted to study and reach my potential, so I chose to bridge my native culture and the one from my new home. When I saw the positive results created by balancing the two cultures, I knew I belonged."

One of the most important steps she took was to become educated. "I knew that if I could get a college degree, I would have a better quality of life. I wanted to do more than just get by or make ends meet; I wanted to make a difference in people's lives. I wanted to make a difference in my daughters' lives." Margarita received a degree in computers and business administration. Her oldest daughter, Jannette, is now attending college and also wants a degree in business administration. Her younger daughter, Dianna, is in elementary school but also has college aspirations.

> "When I saw the positive results created by balancing the two cultures, I knew I belonged."

Margarita and her husband are teaching the girls to be proud of their Mexican heritage: "We visit Mexico, and the girls appreciate the customs my husband and I grew up with. They know the Mayan customs and the ones from Yucatán, and we mix in the American customs and it all works well. I tell them that in order to appreciate where one is at the moment, one has to admire where one came from."

Margarita teaches computer classes to other Latino immigrant adults. A large part of her successful cultural integration is her enthusiastic, positive attitude: "We embrace change and commit to trying new things. For example, I make the time get to know my daughters' American friends so they are allowed to have a sleepover at their house, which is not something I grew up with."

Margarita's daughter, Jannette, struggled with the balance between the two cultures, but she is making progress. "As a teenager I had a lot of temptations typical of that age," said Jannette, "but growing up in a home where modern society and strong family values do not mix, made it more difficult to break the rules." One time in high school when a group of friends were going to have a party, Jannette planned on going until she found out that the party was during school hours: "I could just hear my mom in the back of my head going on and on about how she raised me better than that. Of course, my friends gave me a hard time, but I was too afraid of my mother. It ended up being a good thing because all the kids got a detention for ditching and I didn't!" It took a while for Margarita's daughters to find a balance between the old ways and the new ways, but, as they grew older, they understood why it was important for their mother to preserve her native culture.

Yvonne's Story: I Stuck to My Family's Values but Took the Best from Both Worlds

Yvonne came to this country from Peru almost thirty years ago. She was in her twenties then, and came in search of a better life. With no family here, it was hard for Yvonne to adjust at first. What she learned about herself was that the values she'd been raised with would provide her with the strength she needed to forge ahead in her new environment. "The morals, values, and principles that were instilled in me when I was young have never left me, ever. When I was trying to adjust to a new country or when I became a parent and would question my parental abilities, those deeply ingrained values rose to the surface to remind me of who I am," she said.

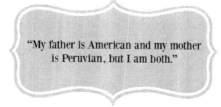
"My father is American and my mother is Peruvian, but I am both."

Yvonne grew up in a strict environment. Even when she questioned her parents, she never did so out loud, only to herself. As she grew older, she was grateful for having been raised in a more conservative home: "The values my parents raised me with made me believe that I am a contributor rather than a taker—in my personal as well as other aspects of my life." Yvonne was determined to contribute to this country. From her very first paycheck, she paid her taxes. She believes she was able to adjust to the American culture by accepting that other people could do as their principles dictated, as could she: "Oh, I could have taken jobs where I could get paid under the table and not pay taxes. But my principles never allowed me to consider this. I wasn't eager to judge others, but I chose to act the way my parents taught me. I basically took the good from both cultures and put them together." That is how she and her ex-husband raised their daughter, who is now twenty-five years old.

"My daughter is well adjusted," says Yvonne. "She values her Peruvian family, despite the fact that she's only seen them a handful of times. She knows that a phone call from her means the world to her ailing grandparents. On her wedding day, it was important for her to have her Peruvian relatives there." Yvonne's daughter, Natalie, agrees. "Being raised in a bicultural home allowed me to define myself as a person," said Natalie. "My father is American and my mother is Peruvian, but I am both. I don't think I understood the benefits of this upbringing until I was in high school, and I think about it now that I am married and want to have a family. My mom was more strict than my dad, as there were things that weren't considered appropriate for a high school-age girl in Peru, but were the norm here, like going to parties and dating." But Natalie learned to balance and respect both ways of parenting. "If anything, it gave me the chance to stay out of trouble!" she said. Natalie is proud to be half Peruvian. "I respect the family unit that my Peruvian family has and wish that for my own family. I want my children to be bilingual and to learn how to appreciate Peruvian foods and customs. I speak in Spanish as often as I can and plan to do so with my kids." Today, Natalie and her husband have a one-year-old son. They are raising him bilingual and bicultural: "I see how my cousin, who was raised here like me and married an American, has totally embraced her Spanish upbringing and is finding ways to teach her children both cultures. That is what I want for my son too."

Dan's Story: My Uncle's Song Taught Me How Mexican-Americans Have Struggled

Dan is second generation Mexican-American. His paternal grandparents were both born in Mexico. "Though I did not live the immigrant experience, I can remember my Uncle Lalo [Lalo Guerrero, father of Chicano music] singing a song about the plight of Mexican-Americans when he was growing up in the United States. The song spoke of his lack of acceptance in this country and the disdain that people had for him when he visited Mexico. He felt disenfranchised in both places. I always remember the sorrow I felt hearing this song about those who had to cope with the lack of identity caused by insensitive people on both sides of the border. I felt that this song could be about me," he said.

He was raised in a town where diversity was a way of life. Growing up, it was not unusual to be exposed to people of many different cultures who celebrated their differences with great pride. They found a balance by holding on to their heritage and finding ways to appreciate their new life here. This created a desire for Dan to learn about his ancestors and his heritage. Spanish was spoken frequently in Dan's home, since his grandparents didn't speak English and visited often. At the same time, Dan's parents instilled in him core values: make sure you get a good education, set goals for yourself, and don't give up on your dreams.

His own children are half Mexican and half Italian, and they were raised to value both cultures—enjoying the food, music, language, and history of each. Though not an immigrant, Dan said he can relate to the concept of being an underdog: "I had to climb the ladder in a profession where people who looked like me were not found in positions of prominence." As the Athletic Director for the University of California, Los Angeles, Dan fought many stereotypes to rise to his present career level: "I was always taught, primarily by my parents, to value education and to always set my sights a little beyond my grasp. My parents encouraged me to seek to be the best, so I never allowed the color of my skin be a deterrent."

Valentina's Story: A Costa Rican with a Red, White, and Blue Heart

Valentina is half American and half Costa Rican. Living in the United States most of her formative years, she grew up considering herself an American. "Our home was kept in the best of high society Costa Rican standards, where Mom cooked and cleaned better than anyone I know. Spanish was spoken at home, and the English-speaking world usually came through the radio, television, or school. I don't remember open conversations about culture in my home," she said. Valentina never really understood why some kids didn't want to come to her house or why her parents didn't agree to send her away to summer camp like so many of her friends'. "The closest I ever got to summer camp was being a Girl Scout and camping out less than a mile away from home," she said.

In her view, keeping a balance was never an issue. Her father always told her and her siblings that they were Americans and part of the best country in the world, to which her mother would usually huff, "We are also Costa Ricans!"

Valentina moved to Costa Rica at twelve years of age, back to the United States at eighteen, and returned to Costa Rica at twenty-two. She was there for fifteen years before returning to the U.S., where she has lived since. "To this day, I only hold a U.S. passport. As a person with two cultures, I've often felt privileged to be able to speak to so many people about Central America, taking on the role of a sort of ambassador. This has opened up many doors for me, often times leading to work, given my language skills. The downside is that people don't understand how a person can have one foot on each continent, which is one of the reasons I chose not to have dual citizenship. My heart has always been red, white, and blue, despite my brown skin," she said.

Valentina is still looking for a balance between the two cultures.

Divorced since her children were four years old, she raised her children, now grown, as a single parent: "I have succeeded in raising my children bilingual and bicultural. Looking back now, worse times were definitely in our first year here, not understanding the U.S. system, feeling so lost, just flat *out of place* all the time; it wears the spirit down. Being constantly confused as undocumented immigrants was also unpleasant, but I attribute this to people's ignorance," she said.

Valentina likes to dwell on the good times: "Hearing my kids speaking so comfortably in English and carrying full-blown conversations, sometimes with perfect strangers, reminds me of how my heart belongs to this country. One day, this woman asked my son what state he was from, she was so surprised to hear him answer, in perfect English, that we were from Costa Rica!"

Claudya's Story: Cultural Pride Starts at Home

Claudya was born in the United States. Her parents are from Mexico. Her mom came from the town of Mexicali, which is very close to the U.S. border. She followed Claudya's father to Northern California where he was working. At the time, there were many Latinos in the area, but Claudya's mom still felt isolated. She missed her family, and there were limited Spanish language radio and television channels, staples of her culture.

Claudya grew up bilingual and bicultural. Her mother fiercely held on to her Mexican roots. The home language was Spanish. English was learned at school. "I love being bilingual and bicultural," Claudya said. "I think it has contributed to the best parts of who I am and has given me a perspective that I wouldn't have otherwise."

Claudya believes that culture is not static, that every generation gets to have a say, but there are some tweaks that may cause cultural clashes along the way: "I was raised by a single mom who usually ended up getting the last say, but it's not like I didn't do plenty of arguing to get her to let me do certain things the 'American' way. I'm not sure if there was balance, but there was a lot of give and take."

Claudya is raising two daughters who are multicultural, and she is doing her best to encourage and motivate their bilingualism. "Right now, getting my children to be fluent in Spanish is a big challenge. Their father is not Latino and does not speak Spanish, so I'm the only one at home trying to get them to speak Spanish," she said. To help, she found a dual immersion public school near her house. "Language is important, but I want them to form their own identity. I am sharing the culture I was raised with, but they aren't just Latinas, they are mixed, so I want them to embrace everything that they are," she said.

In terms of discipline, Claudya is not as strict as her mother was; "I am not the *Mejicana* that my mother is, I am Mexi-merican, or American-Mexican if you will. I am very much a product of the United States." She considers herself more liberal than her mother. "We do not parent alike in many ways. I think about the decisions I make as a parent much more than my mother did. I believe she went with gut and tradition, whereas I go with gut and reasoning. My mother saw me as a direct reflection of her and tried to mold me into the kind of person she thought would be best. I don't see my daughters that way. I don't think it's my job to turn them into something they are not. I think it is my job to help them realize their potential," she said.

Claudya's children are still very young. One is in elementary school and the other is in preschool. She is instilling a love of learning in them and encouraging their strengths because she believes that everyone is smart, and that it's just a matter of finding where that intelligence is focused. "It's funny because I am a huge proponent of education and thought I would be a very academically demanding parent, but I'm not. I want them to learn, but I want them to enjoy the process. I want them to pursue learning in areas that excite them. I want them to find what makes them happy," she said.

Claudya is proud of her heritage. She celebrates it and claims it: "I really believe that's all I have to do for my children to be proud. It's all my mother did, and I can tell you that I have never been ashamed of my heritage because my mother didn't teach me to be ashamed and even when others acted like being 'Mexican' was a bad word, I knew their perception had to do with them and not me at all. I want the same for my children!'"

Success Story: Tony Plana

Tony Plana is a renowned television and movie actor, whose credits include the ABC Family television drama *The Fosters*, as well as four seasons as Ignacio Suárez, the widowed father to America Ferrera's *Ugly Betty*, a groundbreaking series for ABC for which he received a number of international and national awards. *Ugly Betty* was the first Spanish-speaking television series to be adapted to English for a major American network. The show received the highest ratings and was the most critically acclaimed Latino-based show in the history of television.

Tony was educated at Loyola Marymount University in Los Angeles, where he earned a bachelor degree through the honors program in literature and theater arts. He received his professional training at the Royal Academy of Dramatic Arts in London, England.

Before Tony became a famous actor, he was an immigrant child. He was eight years old when his mother and younger brother, Victor, boarded a plane from Cuba to Miami, leaving his father behind. "I came home from school and my mother said, 'We are going to lunch in Miami,'" remembers Tony. "The year was 1960, and the situation in Cuba had gotten worse. My father was concerned about our safety. My family was one of the lucky ones that were able to leave without constraints. At the time, my brother and I thought we were going on a vacation." Tony's mom had packed two suitcases, some money, cigars, all her jewelry, and rum. "Little did I know that our going out to lunch would last fifty years!"

Tony's father, José Vicente, held a high position at a bank in Havana. He was known as a respectful, socially conscious man. He was always involved in some Catholic youth program and in projects that serviced the poor. He was not known for criticizing the government, so he posed no threat to the current Cuban dictator Fulgencio Batista or Che Guevara, whose regime was overtaking the country. Three months after his family left, José Vicente petitioned and was issued permission to leave the country. He left the country with one change of clothes, the hope that the revolution wouldn't last long, and that he and his family would be back.

According to Tony, the hopes of going back became less entertained after the Bay of Pigs, known as the unsuccessful invasion to Southern Cuba by a CIA-trained force of Cuban exiles supported by the United States. Staying in Miami meant sharing a two-bedroom/one-bathroom house with thirteen other people and eating mostly refugee-center food—powdered milk, powdered eggs and Spam. "To this day, I can't look at Spam without thinking of those days," he said.

Tony and his family relocated to Southern California in 1962. They ended up in the Culver City area of Los Angeles. "Culver City and Palms became the cultural hangout for Cuban exiles. The barbershop on Main Street was the place to hang out and talk politics. It was owned by one of my uncles, Gerardo," he said. His other uncle, José, opened up the first Cuban market in the area, El Camaguey. "The store is still there today as is Versailles restaurant, the first to offer authentic Cuban food in L.A.," said Tony. All the Cuban kids ended up in the same elementary and high school. "That area became our home away from home," he said.

Still, Tony was old enough to remember his second grade teacher back in Cuba. She was the first person who stimulated his stage presence. "My teacher selected me to recite poems by José Marti in a musical presentation. That was the first time I performed in front of people. That experienced stayed with me," he said.

By eighth grade, his American teacher was having him do skits for class, and in his sophomore year in high school, he was reading American history documents in front of others and participating in debate competitions and dramatic interpretations. In college, he began to realize that he had a talent for acting and found his true calling: "Honestly, it took me awhile to accept. I was a Cuban firstborn. I didn't see a lot of us on television or the movies at that time. But my teachers saw my potential and they encouraged me. The rest is history."

Tony's first successful theatrical role was as President Kennedy's assassin, Sirhan Sirhan. In his first television role, he was cast as an Arab for an episode of the show *What's Happening?* It was the film *Zoot Zoot* that launched his movie career. Then came roles for over 70 movies, including *An Officer and a Gentleman*, and more than nine television series, including the award-winning show *Ugly Betty*. Tony attributes his successful career to his education and training, as well as his flexibility and adaptability. "I have been open to playing all different kinds of characters and ethnicities," he said. "I have played dramatic roles, comedy, and satirical comedies. That has made my career more versatile and has allowed me to showcase my adaptability and God-given talents."

Tony met his Mexican-born wife, Ada, at an acting class. They have been married for over twenty-four years, and they have two children, Alejandro and Isabel. Family is the most important thing for Tony. "They are the center of my life, and my source of strength, stability, and inspiration. I am a better and more efficient artist because of my family," he said. Tony is also proud of being bilingual, fluent in Spanish and English, and bicultural.

Tony and Ada have raised their children with three cultures: American, Cuban, and Mexican. They have exposed their children to the foods loved by their Cuban and Mexican grandparents, so the children grew up very close to both sets of grandparents. "My children carry a real sense of themselves as cultural people.

> "At the Plana home, the holidays are a fusion of cuisines, or "hybrid" holidays: tamales, ham and pork for Christmas, and they add turkey on Thanksgiving."

They are very aware of their heritage, where they come from, who they are, and who their ancestors are," he said. At the Plana home, the holidays are a fusion of cuisines, or "hybrid" holidays: tamales, ham and pork for Christmas, and they add turkey on Thanksgiving. Tony said: "Holidays, weddings, baptisms, and birthdays, they are all family and extended family and friends celebrations." Tony's children are well read in Latino literature. His daughter, Isabel, is named after the famous Latina author, Isabel Allende. "My family is the typical L.A. melting pot, mixed marriages, multicultural, and multi-lingual. I often joke about us Latinos, we are EOL—Equal Opportunity Lovers! Our families are enriched by many cultures."

After almost half a decade away from Cuba, Tony and his brother, Victor, visited the island. Their aunt was very sick and needed medication brought to her from the States. "It was wonderful to visit the places where I grew up, but also very painful," Tony said. "There is so much suffering still there. It was a bittersweet experience."

Tony said that going back to Cuba reminded him of how his Cuban forefathers influenced the person he is today. "From Cuban national hero and poet José Marti, to political activist and pacifist Amalio Fiallo, to my father and my uncles, they all taught me to be the best I can be and to be responsible for the world around me. To me, this means that whether we are here or we are there, we all have to take a leadership role in society, especially one that took us in when we had none," he said.

Tips for Latino Parents for Balancing Two Cultures

1. Teach your children Spanish. They may complain about having to learn another language, but language is one of the key ways to stay connected to your native country and your relatives back home.

2. At the same time, teach your children English. This is especially important before they go to school in the U.S. or if they are already enrolled. If you are not fluent in English, seek help from your local schools, church, or library.

3. Whenever you have the chance, explain the benefits of being bilingual. They are enormous! There is more information on this in Chapter 4.

4. Celebrate both Latino and U.S. holidays in your home, and explain the origin of each so that your children understand

why it is important to you and to that culture.

5.   Continue to serve traditional foods at your American table, and introduce these foods to your children's friends and their families. Food is a wonderful way to honor culture and to share it.

6.   If you are able, visit your native country and show your children the things you cherish about your original home. There is more about the ups and downs of going home in Chapter 8.

7.   Sit down with your children and develop a plan of action that helps the family find a balance between the two cultures. Consider education, food, clothing, music, holidays, and vacations. Be open to American ways, but be strong in holding onto your heritage. Both pieces of the puzzle are important to find balance.

My Parenting Journal

Successfully raising bicultural children begins with you! You began the process of acculturation the moment you emigrated to this country. It is your example that your children will follow when struggling to fit in or feel accepted. As you reflect on the stories you just read and compare them to yours, write down your feelings and concerns. Here are some questions to get you started.

1.   How well am I adjusting to this country myself? Do I feel like I belong here? If not, do my children know how hard I'm trying to belong?

2.   Am I doing all I can to preserve my native culture in my own life?

3.   Am I making the effort to learn English? If not, what is holding me back?

4.   What am I doing to teach my children to value American culture?

5. What am I doing to show my children that they belong here?

6. What am I doing to teach my children to value my native country's culture?

7. What am I doing to show my children that they belong there, too?

8. Am I teaching my children to look to other successful Latinos who are influential and are making an impact in the United States?

PARENTING IN AMERICA

Chapter 4: Building a Culture of Education at Home

"It is hard for my parents to come to my school and talk to my teachers because their English isn't so good. They never finished high school, but they want me and my brothers to get a good education. It's the main reason we came to America."
—Miguel, age 14

My father always said that when he died, the most important legacy he wanted to leave his children was a good education. I think most parents feel the same way, regardless of their cultural background. For Latino immigrants, providing their children with educational opportunities unavailable back home is one of the main reasons for coming to America.

When a person is educated, regardless of his socioeconomic background, he feels confident and knowledgeable. He can have a conversation about anything and not feel intimidated by the topic or by the person he is talking with. He feels a greater sense of self-respect, and has many more career options.

Education means power, and the majority of immigrant parents I talked to want their children to get a higher education than they did. They want more for them than working at a factory or at a restaurant. They want their children to go to grammar school, finish high school, and go to college because children in America can do that.

A large percentage of Latino immigrants were only able to go to grammar school, and many did not finish high school. School might have been the least important in our minds and lives in our country of origin. We had to work at a young age, and we had to help our families. Education was not paramount to survive. But now, we are in America, and we want more for our children. We have the desire and determination to see our kids do well in school and go on to pursue a higher education. Despite our hopes, however, many Latino parents feel intimidated by the process of American education. It seems complex and confusing, and of course, it is based entirely on a language we didn't grow up speaking.

Regardless of your level of education or your knowledge of the English language, you *can* help your children stay in school and go on to college by building a culture of education at home. Whether they are just beginning preschool or are already in middle or high school, your input is critical.

> "Regardless of your level of education or your knowledge of the English language, you can help your children stay in school and go on to college by building a culture of education at home."

Learning a New Language

Many immigrants did not speak English when they moved to this country. Most did not finish grammar school in their native country, so learning a new language was especially hard. For others, it was more a question of not having enough time to take English classes. Immigrants often hold two jobs until they find one that pays enough. They need to earn enough to send money home, so their families can join them here. Learning a new language is simply too great a task to fit into their already busy schedules.

Those who put off learning English might feel comfortable in communities where everyone speaks Spanish. We may stay close to family and perhaps a few friends from back home. We might find a church where the services are held in our language and watch Spanish language television. By living in a Spanish-only world, we justify our lack of interest in learning English.

Yet, we are adamant about our children learning English and simultaneously polishing their Spanish grammar. We tell them that education is one of the best gifts this country has to offer—and this is true—but we don't take advantage of these opportunities ourselves.

Instead of finding the time to attend English classes, we depend on our English-speaking children to be our eyes, ears, and words. Is that fair to our children? Do we ever stop and think about how it affects them? Aren't we sending them a mixed message?

The Advantages of Speaking Two Languages

There are many advantages to speaking two languages. Some of these advantages have to do with the *acquisition* of language. It's much easier to learn a second language at a very young age. Many other benefits, however, extend far beyond the learning of the language itself. According to the Multilingual Children's Association (multilingualchildren.org) some of these longer-lasting advantages include the following:

- Multilingualism has been proven to help children develop superior reading and writing skills.
- Multilingual children tend to have overall better analytical, social, and academic skills than their monolingual peers.
- Knowing more than one language helps children feel at ease in different environments. It creates a natural flexibility and adaptability, and increases their self-esteem and self-confidence.
- Career prospects are multiplied many times over for people who know more than one language.

Perhaps the most important advantage in teaching your child your native language is that doing so will greatly reduce their overall stress and directly lead to academic and cultural success. David Aguayo, a doctoral student in the Department of Educational, School, and Counseling Psychology in the College of Education at the University of Missouri, recently conducted a study of 408 Mexican-American immigrant students. He found that students who practice speaking their native language did

> "Students who practice speaking their native language did much better in school than students who were only exposed to the English language."

much better in school than students who were only exposed to the English language. "It's a simple correlation, but living and learning within your cultural heritage is a benefit," Aguayo said. "It could be speaking the language in school, eating certain foods, or interacting with other people who share your heritage. The stress level of being in a new culture will decrease if these students have a support system in school, while they adjust to other cultures."

Let's take a look at the specific benefits that some immigrant families enjoyed once they broke through the language barrier. Their stories reveal how they not only insisted upon learning a critical skill, but used the experience as a tool to instill in their children a love of education.

Cristina's Story: Alone in Her Quest to Learn English but Not Alone in the World

Cristina is the oldest of five Mexican-American children. Both her parents, José de Jesús and Juana, grew up on a farm where money was scarce. They came from large families, where the older children were expected to help with household chores, take care of their younger siblings, and work the fields to earn money for the family. Education was considered a luxury they couldn't afford.

When they got married, all Cristina's parents could think of was that they wanted more for their future children. "One thing my parents have always been passionate about is education," said Cristina. "In Mexico, my mother only finished three years of school and my father only one. As a result, my mom came to value education even more passionately. She knew education was a way out of poverty."

Cristina's mother, Juana, learned limited English. When she first moved to the U.S., she took an English as a Second Language or ESL class, but then she became pregnant with Cristina. Soon, the business of raising five children prevented Juana from resuming classes. "She could have done so much better in life if she had learned to speak English," Cristina said. "But after a while, she got comfortable in her zone. She found a job where she didn't need to speak English, and that was the end of it." Her mother was not able to help with homework, but was there to support Cristina and her siblings every step of the way: "My mom would take us to school, smile at the teacher, and continue on her way. She trusted our teachers, and she just handed us over to them. Language was a barrier, so she wasn't engaged. As a parent myself, I recognize the value of engaging in your child's education, but Mom's faith substituted that. At home, she kept reminding us of the importance of an education."

There were times, though, when Cristina wished her mother had been able to help her with certain tasks—like studying for important tests and filling out applications for college. "I got so frustrated that she couldn't help me," she said. "On the other hand, when I did my homework, she would do little things that made a big difference for my siblings and me. She would bring me food and sit with the rosary and pray. How could I bring home a grade lower than an A when my mom prayed for me? How was I going to look her in the eyes if I didn't pass a test after she had so devotedly helped to cut the flashcards in half and copy words onto them so I could study? We owed everything to our parents, and the only way to repay them was with our report card.

"As for my dad, he was focused on being the breadwinner. Even though he had learned enough English to communicate, he couldn't help us much with schoolwork as he was at work most of the time. But he was as passionate about education as my mom, and there was no question in their minds that my siblings and I were going to finish high school and go on to college. Dad would spend his time teaching us valuable lessons, such as surrounding ourselves with successful people to get ahead in life, doing the right thing even when you think no one is looking, and thanking the hand that feeds you."

How did things work out for the family? Juana and Jose raised five children. All of them graduated from college—Loyola Marymount University, University of Southern California, Occidental College, and Brown University—and three of them hold master's degrees from Stanford, UC Berkeley, and Loyola Marymount University. As for Cristina, she is passing on her parents' passion of education to her two young daughters and is engaged in their education on multiple levels. She has committed to work with youth who share a similar tradition, culture, and language as hers.

Veronica's Story: Inspired by Her Mother's Inability to Speak English

Veronica was eight years old when she arrived in America. Like Cristina, her parents are also from Mexico and had very little education. "My parents have always taught me the importance of education," said Veronica. "They use themselves as an example of what not having an education will deprive you of, and, have thus, encouraged me to make the most of myself. While I think my grandparents in Mexico valued education, it wasn't as attainable or as fundamental as it is here." Veronica's mom struggled to adjust to this country, its language, and its customs, but she is supportive of her daughter's goals for a higher education.

Veronica's mother, Patricia, did not learn how to speak English for a long time. "She was not able to communicate with my siblings' teachers, and that frustrated her. I took on the role of guardian of my siblings. That was a problem sometimes because I was busy with my school and my work, and I couldn't always be there for her."

Yet, Veronica believes her mother was in the toughest position of anyone in the family. Veronica's father, Humberto, lived in the U.S. as a teenager, so he learned to speak English. He went back to Mexico, but already knew the language when he returned to the U.S. "For my mother, our move here was a new experience. She was very attached to her family and was forced to leave her world to come here. I feel like it affected her psychologically," Veronica said. Patricia tried to learn the language and attended school for a couple of years, but because of a lack of emotional support from the family, she gave it up. Veronica believes her mother felt isolated and unappreciated.

Americans who speak only English too often assume that immigrants who don't know the language are uneducated. That is not so in Patricia's case. She earned a vocational degree in secretarial work in Mexico. In fact, Patricia had more schooling than Manuel, who attended eleventh and part of twelfth grade in the U.S., but moved back to Mexico before graduating. He has always regretted that. Veronica said, "He sees now that you need a good education in order to get a good paying job. My dad worked two jobs for many years to make ends meet. He doesn't want that for his children."

Veronica believes that having a good education is the key to anything. "American society has made me feel that I need to disprove stereotypes about Latino immigrants' capabilities. I faced many challenges to obtain my college degree. That should mean more than a degree earned by someone born here." Veronica graduated from college with a degree in political science.

Marcy's Story: Mastering America Without Mastering the Language

Marcy was ten when she came to the U.S. from El Salvador to join her mother, Concepción, and stepfather, Jerónimo, who had emigrated a few years earlier. Her mother only finished second grade, and she encouraged Marcy and her sisters to stay in school and to learn English. Marcy was at boarding school back in El Salvador until fourth grade, when she and her sisters joined her parents.

She started sixth grade in Los Angeles, and didn't like school at all. "I guess I was traumatized," she said. "I was in a strange country where people were speaking a language I didn't understand, and I found it hard. I was sad and frustrated and hurt. My mother never told me about this new language!"

After moving to the United States, Marcy's parents always spoke Spanish at home and never English. To this day, her mother manages to find all Latino products for her kitchen. Marcy did not speak English when she arrived, but learned it when she attended elementary school. Her parents never went to school to learn English; they learned enough to get by, but never really speak it that much.

Marcy had a hard time adjusting to school and dropped out in eleventh grade. She found the English language hard, and didn't have many friends. After working in her mother's sewing business for a year, she went back to school to earn her high school diploma. Her parents told her that if she wanted to pursue a higher education, they couldn't afford it. Instead, Marcy worked at odd jobs for a while, but she wanted to do more. She had always being interested in beauty school, so she enrolled and earned a degree in cosmetology. Today, Marcy owns a successful barbershop. Her son works in construction, and her daughter graduated from high school and plans to attend a trade school.

Getting Involved in Your Children's School

Experts agree that children do better in school when parents are involved. According to the Center for Public Education, parental involvement has a significant impact on student achievement in the classroom. In fact, research studies have demonstrated that parental involvement can result in higher student achievement, including higher test scores, higher grades, and outstanding teacher ratings.

Even if you don't speak English, it's still important that you do what you can to become involved in your children's school. Maria Casillas, president emeritus of Families in Schools, said, "Without parent voice, schools are not able to improve as much as they need. Parent leaders can ask for special training so that they learn their roles and carry out their responsibilities effectively for the sake of the children."

There are usually parent education classes that help parents understand what their children are studying. Parents who don't speak English can request that translators be made available when meeting with a teacher. Casillas suggests that, at home, parents set high standards and communicate that learning and education are important. "Parents must make sure their children are focused on reading at all times. Having books and newspapers available and engaging in conversations with their children about a story they read together is an excellent way to inspire and motivate children to love reading."

Providing Role Models

Another important way to build a culture of education is through role models. Our children are growing up in a world filled with accomplished Latinos whom they can look up to and emulate—from news anchors like Jorge Ramos to television personalities like

> "Our children are growing up in a world filled with accomplished Latinos whom they can look up to and emulate."

Gina Rodriguez, to corporate executives like Patricia Salas Pineda to the neighbor down the street who is a respected high school teacher. As parents, we need to encourage our children to follow the examples these role models provide—and to dream big.

Where do kids find role models? For Cristina, it was her eighth grade teacher. "She saw my potential and taught me to believe in myself," Christina said. For Veronica, it was her high school counselor: "In addition to my parents, he helped me transition into college, giving me academic, social, and even financial guidance. When I didn't qualify for state or federal financial aid, he set up a fund for me and helped me get started."

Offering examples of people you know—friends, relatives, colleagues—who are reaping the rewards of a good education, gives kids an incentive to do well.

My Story: An Education was Going to be My Inheritance

My father was fifteen when his grandfather died in his arms. There was no doctor to help my dad save the one person he loved the most. In that moment, my father decided he was going to become a doctor one day. My father's family had no means to send him to medical school, but he was determined and very intelligent.

In those days in Puerto Rico, high school students who did well in school, but had little means, were placed in classes that would eventually earn them a diploma in business. My father was on this track. While he was still in high school, his favorite uncle was the first Puerto Rican to die in World War II. He had named my father as the beneficiary of his life insurance. That was the money that would send my father to medical school. My dad added biology to his curriculum in junior year of high school and graduated with two diplomas, one in business and one in biology. Because of his good grades, he earned a full scholarship to college.

My mother finished high school, but did not go to college. She wanted to go to the University of Puerto Rico in San Juan, but my grandfather did not believe children needed to go to school away from home. He wanted my mom to go to the university in Ponce, where they lived. My mom was as stubborn as he was, so she opted to go to a vocational school instead. She worked as a secretary for a while before she got married to my dad, but then started having babies and decided to be a full-time mom. This was the norm for Puerto Rican couples at the time.

Although my mother didn't go to college, she never stopped learning. When my mom finished school, she knew very little English. She learned it by studying with my dad for his medical board exams, which were all in English. She would type his answers for him and quiz him, thereby expanding her vocabulary. By the time I was old enough to go to school, my mother's English was perfect.

When I told my dad where I wanted to go to college, I assumed that, just like my grandpa, my father wouldn't let me go away either. I had never even been allowed to go to sleepovers away from our city, not even to my aunt's home, and she was like my second mother. I told my father the name of the college, he swallowed hard and said, *"Bueno mija, si ahí es donde quieres ir, para allá vas."* ("Okay, darling, if that is where you want to go, you will go there.) I hugged him, we both cried—and I went to Europe for my first two years of college.

Going to college so far away was difficult for a seventeen-year-old young woman who had never been away from home, except with her parents.' Adjusting to my new life took time. There were only two Puerto Ricans at the school. There were a few Americans, and the rest of the students were from somewhere in Europe. The language of communication was English, but most everyone spoke three to four languages. There were so many cultures living together that I lost count. I learned about customs I didn't know existed, and we learned tolerance, acceptance, and respect from each other. The opportunity my father granted me was invaluable, and to this day I am immensely grateful. I continued my education back in Puerto Rico and finished my bachelor's degree there. Then I came to California and earned a master's degree. I will never be able to repay my parents other than to encourage and motivate my own children to pursue high educational goals.

My son always had a clear vision for his career goals. He is passionate about his craft and decided to take time off from college so he could acquire experience and hone his talents and skills in his field. My husband and I believe in him and support his dreams, but we want him to finish his degree. We are confident he will! My daughter is in her senior year of college and will receive a degree in advertising. All four of my parents' children finished college, and both my sister and I received a master's degree. My sister's daughters all finished their degrees and the family now has a doctor, a CPA and a lawyer. Two of my brother's children also finished their bachelor's degree and are both in the retail industry. My oldest brother is a lawyer and my youngest brother is in business. It makes me happy to say that we all fulfilled my father's dream of a good, solid education!

Ana Barbosa' Success Story: Instilling a Love for Learning

Ana Barbosa is a former executive with Southern California Edison. She was twelve years old when she first came to the U.S. from Mexico. Along with her husband of more than forty years, Henry, who is also of Mexican descent, she has raised four daughters, all of them bilingual and bicultural. "We raised our girls pretty much the same way our parents raised us," Ana said. "Above all, there is unconditional love."

Ana's oldest daughter, Analisa, said, "In elementary and junior high school, we were only allowed to watch one television show a week. Each of us could pick one program a week, Monday through Friday. The rest of the time, was spent reading or doing homework. Also, my mom was pretty vigilant about limiting the time we were allowed to spend on the telephone. My sisters and I hated these rules, but eventually we came to understand and accept them."

"Exposure to new ideas generated a curiosity that fueled academic success in all the girls."

Analisa believes that growing up in a highly structured environment greatly contributed to her and her sisters' academic success: "There was breakfast in the morning, school during the day, and a snack ready when we got home from school. There were extracurricular activities after school—usually soccer, catechism, or volunteer work—then dinner, homework, and bedtime. Being able to count on this pattern from Monday through Friday was crucial."

Analisa and her sisters, Cristina, Maricela, and Alejandra, believe that the greatest gift their parents gave them was exposing them to music, art, theater, politics, and history at a very young age. "From the Hollywood Bowl during the summer festival to the Nutcracker at Christmas, to discussions at home about local and national elections, we couldn't get enough," said Analisa. Ana and Henry always looked for ways to inspire the girls intellectually. Exposure to new ideas generated a curiosity that fueled academic success in all the girls.

Since Ana and Henry are avid readers, the girls emulated their behavior. There were also incentives. In the summer, the family would go to the library, and Ana would offer the girls a dollar for every book they read or a quarter for every article they read in the newspaper. "We would have to write a couple of sentences about the article to prove we read it, but in those days, that was big money and worth the reading!"

said Analisa.

Today, Analisa and her sisters are all college graduates with successful careers. Analisa graduated from Yale University, Cristina from Columbia University, Maricela from Boston College, and the youngest, Alejandra, attended Princeton. "We owe our parents a great debt," said Analisa. "It was their love, encouragement, patience, and good example that helped us be who we are today. We are living proof that anything is possible with a good education."

Tips for Latino Immigrants to Build a Culture of Education at Home

1. Motivate and encourage your children to learn from the minute they are born. Play games to make learning fun, ask questions to prompt curiosity and analytical thinking, and encourage children to participate in hands-on learning opportunities such as counting silverware when setting the table, measuring ingredients when preparing meals, or reading instructions for a recipe.

2. You can create a culture of education in your own home by being a good example and by looking for ways in which you can improve yourself. If you don't speak English, find an ESL (English as a Second Language Class). Look for these at your community center, church, or even at the neighborhood elementary school. Some of these classes are offered at night or on the weekend, and some might be free of charge.

3. Limit the number of video games or toys you give to your children and turn off the television. Instead, buy them books and find ways to instill the love of reading. Start by getting a library card. It's free and there are plenty of books to look at, even if you can't read. You and your child can both look at the pictures and learn from that. Most libraries have reading time, where someone reads to the children out loud. Even if it is in English, this can foster a love of learning.

4. Always check out a book for yourself when you visit the library. The more books you read, the more likely your children will read too.

5. Attend every PTA meeting and every parent/teacher conference when your children are in elementary school. Find out everything you can about your children's school, their teachers, the subjects they're studying, and how they are doing in their classes. Don't assume your child is doing well. Ask questions and try to stay involved. If there are other parents at your child's school who don't speak English fluently, get together with them and the school officials to enlist the services of a translator for PTA meetings and parent/teacher conferences.

6. When your child is in middle school, find out how to get them on track to get into college. Talk to counselors, teachers, and anyone else at their school who might offer suggestions and help.

7. Provide your children with examples of successful, educated, bilingual Latinos. One way to do this is to subscribe to *Latina Style* magazine, which often features accomplished Latinas. If you cannot afford a subscription, ask your local library to add it to their collection. Read every issue and share the articles with your children.

8. Make a list of additional things you can do to help your children do well in school. Discuss the list with your children. They might have things to add to your list.

My Parenting Journal

Write down the thoughts and feelings that came to mind as you were reading this chapter. The following will help you get started.

1. How might your own background and educational

experiences inspire your children? Consider sharing your stories of both successes and failures with your kids.

2. Have you accepted that it is important for you to be actively involved in your child's education? If not, what might be holding you back?

3. If you don't speak English, are you enrolled in ESL classes? If not, why not?

4. Are you enrolled in parenting classes? If so, how are they helping you to take a more active role in your child's education? If not, how do you think such classes might encourage you to take a more active role in your child's education?

5. Are you attending all PTA and parent-teacher meetings at school, even if you can't communicate well? Just showing up is an important way to show your children that their education matters to you.

6. Have you made an appointment to meet with your high school student's counselor to discuss college options? Academic requirements? Financial aid? The sooner you make the appointment, the better chance your child has at successfully applying to college.

Chapter 5: Why Can't I Raise My Kids the Way My Parents Raised Me?

"I grew up in a different world. It was my parents' way or no way. They raised us with strong morals values, and I never questioned them. It is different here. I like that, but I still believe that those strong convictions shape the person that I am today. Even if there are things I am willing to do different as a parent, I tend to go back to the way I was raised."
—Teresa, age 42

Parenting is the most rewarding of life's experiences, but it is a difficult job no matter where we live or what our circumstances are. Adding immigration to the mix only makes parenting harder. Whether one's first home was Mexico, El Salvador, Columbia, Cuba, Argentina, or Puerto Rico, Latino immigrants grew up within a culture that has its own strong set of principles. Among others, these include respect for elders, responsibility and accountability for one's actions, a firm sense of right versus wrong, devotion to religion, loyalty to family above all, honesty and compassion, and the belief that hard work is the key to building a strong character.

> "When we make the choice to come to America and raise our children here, we must accept that there is, perhaps a more flexible way to parent."

Americans also have a strong set of values, many of which are similar to those held by Latinos. But the way they go about living those values might be slightly less structured than the way Latinos do. Latinos usually allow no exception to the rules. For example, our reverence toward elders means that we don't question their word or argue with them; we simply accept their pronouncements and do what we are told. Some might say that Latinos grow up with authoritarian parents.

Others might argue that this attitude is partly the result of how some Latin countries were run by authoritarian governments. This might be true, but our unwavering respect for our elders is an integral part of who we are.

Our values also define who our children will become. However, when we make the choice to come to America and raise our children here, we must accept that there is, perhaps a more flexible way to parent. Our children did not ask to come here. We brought them here or they were born here, so we must be the ones to help them adjust to the American way of life.

Accepting new ways of parenting doesn't mean we cannot honor our roots. As we explore the American way of raising kids, consider the following strengths and challenges inherent in Latino culture, and think of how they might influence your style of parenting.

The Strengths

- Immigrant parents were generally raised with strong values that they use to guide their children in America's culturally diverse society.
- Immigrant parents were raised with a strong sense of respect for adults and parental authority, which can be critical in shaping a child's character.
- Immigrant parents have a strong motivation and resolve to preserve their customs and cultural heritage.

The Challenges

- Immigrant parents don't feel confident in their new country and may lack a sense of authority with their children.
- Two hardworking immigrant parents might not have sufficient time or energy to devote to their parental obligations.
- Immigrant parents are more reluctant to ask for help when raising their children.

Immigrant Parenting Strengths and Challenges

Latino children have the best of both worlds. They are raised with strong values, yet they are also taught that life might not be as black and white as it was for *mami* and *papi*; there are gray areas to consider. This can be a challenge for some immigrant parents who may fear that straying from the way our parents raised us can result in forgetting where we came from. Perhaps we need to look at our stage of immigrant adjustment and think about how that might affect our ability to parent our kids.

If we haven't fully adjusted to our new country, we may not feel very self-assured. A lack of confidence in one's self can lead to a lack of parental authority. "How can I not have authority at home?" we may ask ourselves. We think about our own parents, who never seemed to waver in their authority. What we tend to forget is that we are struggling with challenges our parents didn't have. Not only do we work hard, we're also adjusting to new customs and values, and trying to raise our family in a new country. When we fail to fully succeed in each of these areas, our self-image suffers. This is especially the case if we don't speak the language, while our children are becoming more fluent.

For most immigrant parents, there is another challenge to consider: being too busy to adequately parent our kids. Very often, immigrant parents have multiple jobs, or both parents work outside the home, so children may return from school to an empty house. Kids who are new to this country may find this challenging. They were used to grandparents or other family members always being home. There, they were always told what to do; here, no one is around to guide them. This can be scary and confusing for children.

Immigrant parents often hold on to the parenting values of "back home," and this can present additional problems. We need to accept that our lives and our children's lives have changed dramatically. Then we can help them understand the changes to make them feel secure and confident within their two worlds.

How Does the Immigration Experience Affect How We Parent?

In addition to my story, here are three stories about what happens to families when they move to this country. See if you can relate to their experiences and if you have been able to find a balance within your own parenting styles.

Consuelo and José: We Learned How to Listen to Our Children

When we last read about Consuelo, she was having a hard time because she did not speak English. Yet she and her husband, José, were determined to reunite with their children, ages ten and five, so she worked hard to learn the language and get a better job. She went from being a cleaning lady to working as a nanny, and along the way, had a baby. Her husband found a steady job in a restaurant. Since it was a hardship to travel, they visited Mexico only twice to see their children. When they finally had enough money, they sent for their children. Their dream was becoming a reality! At that point, however, they weren't thinking about the parenting challenges they would face once their children were in the U.S.

After a brief period of confusion, the older children quickly adopted certain American ways. The oldest boy, Daniel, started wearing baggy pants and had his ear pierced so he could wear an earring. Daniel didn't come home after school like he was told and constantly questioned family rules. He wasn't doing his schoolwork, and never wanted to be with the family.

All three children wanted to speak only English at home. Then their ten-year-old son, Pepito, who had always looked up to his older brother, started to emulate Daniel's attitude and behavior. He decorated his schoolbooks with gang-style calligraphy and constantly talked back to his mother. The baby of the family, Juan, was growing up with television shows like Barney and Pokemón, and he couldn't understand why his mother liked to watch only Spanish-language TV.

Consuelo felt frustrated and helpless, José felt discouraged, and the kids were confused and rebellious. "We want the best for our children," Consuelo said, "but sometimes we don't even know who they are. They are not like the American children I take care of. American children don't disrespect their parents like our children do now. They don't even want to speak our own language! Maybe we made a mistake by bringing them here. Maybe we should have stayed back there."

> "Consuelo and José talked to their friends who had been in this country longer and asked them for advice. Their friends told them to be patient and to talk and listen to their kids more."

Consuelo and José talked to their friends who had been in this country longer and asked them for advice. Their friends told them to be patient and to talk and listen to their kids more. After initially wanting to parent their three sons according to the old ways, Consuelo and José were willing to listen to their kids and compromise. For example, the oldest, Daniel, explained to his parents why it was important for him that his parents trust him and be more flexible. In turn, Daniel would follow curfew rules and be a better example for the younger siblings. He even volunteered to do Spanish homework with the younger boys. Consuelo and José appreciated his efforts and allowed him to go camping with his American friend and his family. Things were not perfect right away, but slowly there were improvements. It was important for the kids to understand why their parents felt strongly about preserving values from their native country, and it was important for the parents to accept that their children could do things differently in the U.S. without disrespecting their culture or their family.

Sylvia and Manuel: Learning to Compromise and Seek Help

It took Sylvia and Manuel five years to bring their kids to America. By then, Sylvia had a steady job with a family that treated her with love and respect. She had also learned some English and felt good about her efforts. Manuel worked really hard at two jobs, but was grateful.

They were both so busy, however, that all they could do when the kids arrived was enroll them at their local school and hope for the best. Too busy to think how or when or if their kids would adjust to their new life, they were just happy to have the family together at last.

"When we were growing up, we never questioned the changes our families went through; we just accepted them, so we figured our kids would do the same," said Sylvia. "But moving to a new country—this change was different; I see that now. Our children must have been terrified of their new environment, and we just didn't know what they were going through. After a few months, the school called to tell us that our children, Luis, twelve, and Beca, nine, were misbehaving and not paying attention. Because they couldn't speak English, other kids were making fun of them. There were a lot of Spanish-speaking kids at the school, but they all spoke English, too, so my kids felt unaccepted. As immigrant parents, we were shy and unable to communicate well with the teacher. We lacked confidence because our English was not so great either. We didn't even know what a PTA was!"

> "We lacked confidence because our English was not so great either. We didn't even know what a PTA was!"

Initially unaware of what living in a new country would require of them as parents, Sylvia and Manuel had to refocus their attention and take a more active role with their children. Given their busy work schedules, this was indeed a challenge, but they found a way. They met with their kids' teachers and, with the help of another teacher who spoke Spanish, talked about the problems their children were having. The teachers made suggestions, and then Sylvia and Manuel went home and talked to their kids. They encouraged and motivated them by talking about how they all felt.

The kids told Sylvia and Manuel how difficult it was for them to be away from their little town and how much they missed their friends. They even admitted that they hated to feel different because they didn't speak English. Sylvia and Manuel offered support and reminded them why they moved away. "This is a better life for us, you need to trust that," Sylvia said. They explained the importance of getting a good education, and that the teacher would help them with the new language.

The family also discussed the old rules and why they were important, and the kids brought up new rules. As the teacher suggested, Sylvia and Manuel agreed to compromise and accept certain new rules. For example, Beca was allowed to go for a sleepover after Sylvia called and met the friend's mother.

My Story

After we got married, my husband and I worked all day and barely came home to sleep. Parenting was the furthest thing from our minds. I was still adjusting to being away from home. To me, California was where we were living temporarily. It was not home. Home was Puerto Rico—until I had my first child. The birth of my son made me feel like I belonged in this country.

When our son was still a baby, we talked about how we would bring him up bicultural and instill the love for both his Puerto Rican and Greek heritage. At that point, discipline and values seemed so far away that we didn't really talk about those issues. We both took for granted that we would raise our children pretty much the same way we had been raised by our parents.

Over the years, however, my husband and I have had many discussions about the values with which we were raised and how they differ from what is taught in America. We have always believed in balance and apply that to our parenting decisions. At times, there are conflicts. We tend to be stricter in our rules and more conservative than most of the parents around our children, so there are arguments and comparisons. For example, my daughter has argued that it is not fair that her curfew is earlier than her friends', who are a year younger. Perhaps she is right, but we still didn't change it. Many times, I say to the kids, "I would have never thought of questioning my parents' decisions or arguing with them as you do with us." And my husband will say, "The answer is 'no'—and there is no discussion about it," just like his dad would have said. Still, we are raising our kids to be free thinkers and to express their opinions, the way children do in this country. So we try to create a sense of balance between the parenting philosophies of *aquí* and *allá* (here and there).

I grew up with lots of rules: no dating until I was eighteen, no sleepovers, no going on field trips organized by the school without my mom, no talking back, and no using bad language. Family always came first, it was important to give back, obedience was a must, honesty was a priority, and one never, ever, compromised one's integrity. In my home, both of my parents were disciplinarians. My mother was a stay-at-home-mom, and she dealt with us during the day. We used to drive her crazy, all four of us, each only one year apart in age. Sometimes, she would lose her temper and spank us, but I know she hated doing that because she would often cry after using the belt. My dad used the belt too, but I only remember him using it twice. We had disobeyed him, and one never disobeyed our dad! Yet, when I look back now, my childhood memories are more about happy times, lots of love, and lots of learning. There was always a value to be learned, and every day we had an opportunity. For example, expressing our gratitude for something a neighbor or a relative did was a must. If we were sent a present for our birthday, we had to send a written thank you card. If our neighbor had dropped off a dessert, we had to call and say thank you.

It was these standards, demanded by my parents and other family members, that made me into the parent I am today. My home is filled with rules, more than my kids' friends' homes, or so they feel. They remind me of this all the time.

In America, parents tend to listen more and use physical punishment less. When a child misbehaves, there is a discussion as to why there is a consequence. Parents are motivated by the desire to teach a lesson rather than by promoting fear.

But I hear my mom and dad when I say, "That is there, this is here."

How many times did I swear I wouldn't be that kind of parent? Do we as immigrant parents wonder and hesitate rather than stay firm and consistent? Do we question our rules because of the lack of time we have to devote to our parental obligations? "We are busy, we both work, we just don't have the time," some might say.

From the music they weren't allowed to listen to, to the movies they weren't allowed to watch, to the online sites they weren't permitted to visit, my

> "In America, parents tend to listen more and use physical punishment less. When a child misbehaves, there is a discussion as to why there is a consequence. Parents are motivated by the desire to teach a lesson rather than by promoting fear."

children grew up with two parents who truly valued their immigrant heritage. We were willing to strike a balance between the way we were raised and the way kids are raised in this country, but we were not willing to compromise our Latino and Greek heritages.

Latino and American Values: How Different Are They?

As immigrant parents in America, we raise our children with two approaches to values: one that we bring to this country and the other that we learn when we get here.

Many of us believe that Latino and American values are separate and unequal. But let's ask ourselves the following: Is working hard and being responsible a Latino value or a universal one? Or being loyal to one's family? Don't most cultures value religion? Maybe there isn't such a difference after all. Perhaps different cultures demonstrate their values differently. For instance, Latinos demonstrate their respect for elders by accepting their word without question while Americans demonstrate it by inviting them to family functions and by communicating via the internet or phone.

We can help our children practice our values while incorporating American values. Teaching our kids to live with integrity—so that values, words, and actions are in sync—is one of the greatest lessons we can convey. Whether we demonstrate our deeply held values in a

Latino, American, or a Latino-American fashion, when we're true to our beliefs, our children will be inspired to be true to theirs.

Milly Quezada's Success Story: Parenting with Two Cultures

For more than twenty years, Milly Quezada has delighted the United States, Puerto Rico, South America, Europe, and her native Dominican Republic, with her music. She is known in the Latin music world as "The Queen of Merengue," *La Reina del Merengue*. Milly knows firsthand what it is like to come to this country and to have to adjust to a new life.

"I was a preteen when I came to the United States, along with my two brothers and sister, Rafelito, Martin, and Jocelyn," she said. "We moved into what was then an all Irish and Italian neighborhood, now known as Washington Heights, a predominantly Dominican neighborhood in New York City. In those days, we struggled to assimilate and played music in our parents' three-bedroom apartment to fight off nostalgia." That was how her group, *Milly & Los Vecinos*, became known.

"My grandmother, mother, and father are now deceased, but we lived as an extended family," she said. "Growing up, we did encounter cultural shock, but our strong religious upbringing helped us stay grounded and away from the natural temptations of the teenage years. Our father also played a key role as the disciplinarian. Our parents were busy, working six days a week supporting us and their relatives back home.

"As a widowed mom to three teenagers, I encountered my own struggles. Circumstances today are different than those I grew up with, so I choose to be more flexible, more communicative, and less disciplinarian. For example, I try to listen to my boys, and allow them room for open discussions, even at the risk of getting disrespected."

Milly believes that having grown up in the U.S. has considerably reduced her capacity to readapt to the Dominican way of life: "I have lived two-thirds of my life in the United States, studied through college, married, settled down, and have borne three wonderful boys here. I don't anticipate going back to the homeland to live. I do anticipate visits and vacationing." One drawback, said Milly, is the thin line that separates the Dominican from the American—a place, at times, uncomfortable, and at other times, beneficial. "I sometimes feel I am here but belong there, and other times when I go there, I feel I belong in America!"

Milly's children were all born in the United States. Miguel is in his late thirties, Anthony in his early thirties, and Rafael in his mid twenties. "They are bilingual and very aware of their Latin American roots, and they love both countries," she said. "While influenced by their American counterparts, they come home to a Dominican mom who gives them another side to the story, one which they can choose to be influenced by or not. That decision is theirs alone to make, one whose consequence they will have to live with.

"Raising my children has been an exciting, challenging, and joyful experience only saddened whenever there has been a rite-of-passage to experience without their dad." Milly's husband of twenty years, Rafael Vázquez, died at the age of forty-four. "My family gathered around me and supported me and my boys one hundred percent. My sister, Jocelyn, a former co-singer and now a pastor, and her husband, Fausto, also a pastor, have provided spiritual support as Christian ministers. I have had a nanny, Argentina, who has loved my boys unconditionally for the past thirty-one years. They call her 'Mom.' Their uncles provided positive male role models in their growing years."

Today Milly is a proud grandmother of two girls, Mia and Maria, representing the second generation of children in her family born in the U.S.: "They, too, are part of my *Arroz con Pollo and Apple Pie* story as they are receiving from me much of the love for merengue music, *arroz con pollo* with Argentinian delights I make for them, and our rich cultural background so they are growing up and living under both influences, the American and the Dominican way!"

To Latino immigrant parents, Milly said, "Courage and faith will move you forward; anything else will distract you and steer you away from your vision. There is a way to raise our kids to love and respect the values embedded in their background while also loving and respecting the American way."

Tips for Latino Immigrant Parents on Parenting with Two Cultures

Consuelo and Jose's, Sylvia and Manuel's, and Milly's stories, illustrate some of the difficulties we immigrant parents have when raising our children. Although we all want the best for them, we often do not realize how deeply they are affected when moving to a new country. Often, in the course of our journey, we feel like Milly, like we're neither here nor there.

Here are parenting tips for you to consider as you attempt to balance the Latino and American ways of raising children.

1. Accept the fact that you were raised with strong moral values and that there is a different way of practicing those values in the U.S.

2. Talk to other immigrant parents about how they are raising their kids. It always helps when you realize that other parents can relate to your situation.

3. Accept that compromise is not bad for your children. Decide where you will compromise and where you will not.

4. Make sure that both parents agree on the way children will be disciplined. Children need to hear the same message from both parents; mixed messages cause confusion.

5. Don't be hard on yourself. Have confidence in your abilities, regardless of the struggles you're currently experiencing.

6. Get involved in your children's education. Go to your child's school and meet the principal and teachers. Talk to them about your children. If there are other Latino children in their schools, these officials and teachers may have experience that is of benefit to you.

My Parenting Journal

If we can adjust to our new life in the U.S. by incorporating certain American ways of thinking and behaving, we can also learn to adjust as parents. Our children will benefit from that positive shift in our parenting philosophy.

On the following blank page, write down the thoughts and feelings that came to mind while you were reading this chapter. Here are some topics that might help you get started.

1.   Do you believe that you are raising your kids with two sets of values or with one set of values that can be interpreted two different ways?

2.   Do you accept that raising your kids with both American and Latino interpretations of your values can be both a challenge and a strength?

3.   Are you generally positive about the challenges of balancing American and Latino styles of parenting, or are you always complaining about the way things are here?

4.   Have you found a way of compromising between American and Latino parenting styles? Explain how.

5.   Do you and your spouse agree on the compromises you have reached? If not, what can you do to foster this agreement?

6.   If you have not found a balance between how Americans and Latinos interpret your values, how is that lack of balance affecting your children? How is it affecting the entire family?

Chapter 6: Discipline: Understanding the American Way

"I hate it when my mom says, 'When I was your age, growing up in Mexico, I had no choices. I never questioned my parents like you do here.' I don't want to have no say in how I live my life, like it was for my mom. It is different here—and I like it better."

—Belinda, age 12

When we become parents, we often become *our parents*—even when we swore we would never follow in their footsteps. After having kids, we find ourselves doing what our parents did and saying what they said. "Finish your meal before you can have dessert." "Finish your homework before you go outside to play." "Help your *mami* do the chores." "Don't talk back to your *papi* or you will be punished."

Although all parents discipline their children in some fashion, the way each culture handles discipline can be quite different. For Latino immigrant parents, the way we were disciplined as children was very different than how American parents discipline their kids. For Latinos, it is considered disrespectful for children to voice their opinion to their parents or other adults. Respect for our elders was the law; if we dared to disobey, we were in a lot of trouble.

In the U.S., parents are open to hearing their child's opinions, explanations, and feelings. Parents still set the rules and dole out consequences when their kids break the rules, but moms and dads here are more willing to listen to their children and to change their minds. The American way doesn't mean that parents and children are on equal footing, it means that parents respect and validate their children as individuals with ideas and thoughts of their own.

Exploring Your Style of Discipline

Here are four stories, including my own, that might help you identify your own style of disciplining your children. As you read these stories, think about the way you were disciplined and how it has impacted the way you are raising your kids.

Maria's Story: Parents Are the Authority

Originally from Honduras, Maria has been in the United States since 1993. She and her husband have four daughters and one son. They live in a small but very happy home in a tough area of Los Angeles. Maria believes their house is blessed. In raising their children, she follows the customs of her native country. "My husband and I are the authority, just like my parents were where I grew up," said Maria. "But we are more understanding than my folks were." Maria and her husband, Mauricio, share discipline duties at home: "If he punishes them for not being obedient or for not listening to what he asked, I respect that. I don't go about lifting punishments. We are in this together, and we have to support each other." But she also believes in listening to her kids' side of the story and explaining the consequences when they misbehave. When Maria was growing up, her parents never offered explanations or gave the children a chance to voice their opinion. "That was just the way it was done. There was no trust in the children; the adult had the rights. Hitting, slapping, and pulling someone by their hair were customary." Though she doesn't use such drastic measures to punish her daughters, Maria never felt resentment towards her parents. "They disciplined us that way because they loved us," she said.

Maria believes in openly communicating with her kids, but she and her husband are strict. For instance, if they misbehave, they do not get to watch TV. If they don't make their beds before leaving the house, they have to do the chore they dislike the most. One of her kids hates to do the dishes, so her consequence is to do the dishes for a week. Maria admits that she will "spank their behinds" if they don't obey.

"There is nothing wrong with a swat when the behavior is out of control," she said. "It worked for my parents. It works for me." She wants them to learn how to behave properly so they won't get into worse trouble when they're older. Maria dramatically illustrates this point when she takes her kids to visit a cousin who is in prison. When one of her children asked why the boy was behind bars, she told all of her kids that the cousin had not obeyed the law and hadn't listened to his parents. She reminded her children that when you go against the rules—or the law—there will always be serious consequences.

Maria accepts that there are differences in the way the two cultures handle discipline, but she believes that raising children with the best of both is important. Her kids are growing up knowing the difference between respect and authority. They respect their parents and also feel respected by them, but they know that their parents have the authority to discipline them. And they accept that.

Antonia's Story: Raised With the Best of Both Worlds

Antonia's mother, Petra, emigrated from Mexico when she was thirteen. She lived with her aunt and initially thought she was in the U.S. just for a visit, but was actually sent here to stay. In school, she had a difficult time because she didn't speak any English and the kids were mean to her. When Petra and her aunt visited Mexico each summer, Petra yearned to stay with her parents, but she dared not question them. She would return to the U.S., saddened by the separation from her family. At twenty-one, Petra married Ramiro, also a Mexican, and they had seven children. Antonia is one of them.

Antonia believes her parents assimilated into American culture fairly well because they came here when they were younger. But, even as adults, they never forgot their roots. They raised their children in a way that reflected both styles of discipline, the Latino way and the American way. "If we didn't obey, we were spanked. My parents were not afraid to use the belt if we had done something extreme. For example, in fifth grade, my sister and I found a pack of cigarettes and decided to try one. We were ten and it was late at night, so we just went to the kitchen, turned the burner on, and one of us burned her hair, so we had to tell! Boy, were my parents disappointed, and they used the belt," she said.

Another time, Antonia said she talked back to her mom, and her brother, who is six years older, slapped her. "I think my mom was startled by his action, but I could tell she was also proud of him for knowing what was right," she said. Antonia was born and raised in this country and feels that her own upbringing affects the way she is raising her young boys: "I will not be afraid to spank with my hands if my boys do something really bad." When her boys were toddlers, she would teach them right from wrong by saying "No" when they walked to the fireplace, for instance, and would remove them from the situation. "I try to be consistent with my messages and that is how they learned," she said. She also used time-outs like they do in America.

In her opinion, teaching her boys to say "please" and "thank you" was the beginning of teaching respect: "When I was growing up, respect was very important to my parents. We showed respect by following the rules and by doing our chores. If a visitor came, we would say hello and disappear. In my generation, children were seen but not heard. My kids have learned to be respectful, but they are heard."

There were times however, when growing up with Mexican parents was difficult. For example, she and her sister had more rules and chores than any of their American friends. "My twin sister and I had to clean our house every Saturday. We did the laundry, and we ironed. My one American friend learned to iron with us. She wanted us to hurry up to play, so she would help us," she said. It wasn't until Antonia was in junior high school that she was allowed to do more fun things with her friends. Her parents were much stricter than any other parents they knew, and "there was no sweet-talking them." One time, a girlfriend asked Antonia to stay out later than her curfew. "I told her there was no way I could disobey my parents, that it wasn't worth getting in trouble. Not only that, but if I came home late, I knew that my parents would worry, and I didn't want to upset them," she said.

Even as a teenager, Antonia knew she had been raised differently than her friends, but she loved and respected her parents: "My parents taught me that respect and love go hand in hand. It is

> "Though they accepted the ways of their new culture, Antonia's parents remained true to the teachings of their own parents."

difficult to have one without the other." Though they accepted the ways of their new culture, Antonia's parents remained true to the teachings of their own parents.

Today, Antonia's boys are almost teenagers. They are being raised bilingual and bicultural. "They look at the world more openly because they know that their blood holds two cultures: my Mexican culture and my husband's Caucasian culture. They have been to a few quinceañeras, birthday parties with mariachis, and enough carne asadas dinners to know that their life is a little different than their friends. They love telling people that I have a hundred-and-ten first cousins because they know that is not the 'norm.' Both cultures have so much to offer, and I feel fortunate to give them those advantages. They live their life in the Caucasian world, but are sprinkled with my Mexican culture and traditions" she said.

Rosa's Story: The American Way Works

Rosa, who emigrated from Mexico over fifteen years ago, has four children, all of whom were born in the United States. They are Mexican-American, and Rosa's style of parenting is somewhat different than her parents. She was raised in a very authoritarian environment in which she did what her parents asked without explanations or complaints. "My kids live in a very Latino environment. We speak Spanish at home, they go to school with almost all Latino kids, and we follow all the customs," said Rosa. "When it comes to discipline, I talk to them and they talk to me. We communicate." But Rosa admits that sometimes there is chaos at home: "I can get really mad if they misbehave. When

I scream at them, they start cleaning or whatever else they need to do or have not done. I tell them that I am working for them and that the least they can do is help me around the house."

Rosa believes she commands respect because she treats her children with respect. "I don't judge the way I was raised. My parents did the best they knew how, but I want my kids to trust me and talk to me. Even though I am the authority, I am also an understanding mom," she said.

Unlike Maria, Rosa doesn't believe that spanking is the way to discipline children. "This is where I draw the line between the two ways of discipline," she said. "Instead of hitting them, I talk to them. When talking doesn't work, I take away privileges, like my American friends do with their kids."

Rosa believes that her children respect her, just as she respected her parents at their age. "But my kids are not afraid of me. We have a good relationship. I like that I can have my kids respect me, and at the same time, I can discipline them in a non-physical way. I see it as the best of both ways of disciplining my kids," she said. Today, Rosa's oldest daughters attend an all-girl high school and they like to speak more English than Spanish, but she continues to encourage the language. She also has a younger daughter that she is raising bilingual and both languages are spoken at home.

My Story: My Upbringing Influenced my Parenting Reality

I grew up an American citizen, but I am Puerto Rican first and American second. My mom and dad had high expectations for their children. They were both born and raised on the island and grew up with very strict rules—especially my mother. She was the youngest of twelve. My grandmother, Mima, was tough. She was a small woman, but no one ever crossed her. One time, we were at her house and my cousin gave my sister a fruit that we were not allowed to eat. A big seed got stuck in her throat and Mima got so mad at my cousin that she spanked her butt, grounded her, then threw the bag of fruit out the balcony! My mom's father was a bit more forgiving. He would ask my mom to sit down and would tell her how disappointed he was in her. "That would make you feel even worse," said my mom. "He'd say he was going to be watching me and that is all it took for me to be obedient."

As a parent, my mother was more lenient than my grandmother. She allowed us to explain why we should be allowed to do something, and, at times, she was our buffer with our dad. But she did use the belt. In those days, the belt was the disciplinary tool of choice. We did get warnings, but often, the misbehaving didn't stop until after the belt was used.

My dad was *the* authority in our house. He had the last word in all things concerning discipline. If my dad said we couldn't go to a party, we didn't go. Disobeying my dad was a rarity. My poor mom got most of our misbehaving—like most mothers do in any culture!

Truth be told, my dad was a softy. There were many times when, on a whim, he would retract a punishment given to us by my mom. As a parent myself now, I realize that negating my mom's disciplinary actions was probably not such a good thing for my dad to do. But it was his way of letting my siblings and I know that he knew we weren't perfect, but still loved us.

I may have not agreed with the use of the belt, but I have fond memories of my childhood. Like most Latino homes, ours was loud and busy. My mom screamed a lot. When she screamed, we shaped up. As we grew older, my mom would listen. She would remind us about the rules, but she would also lobby on our behalf to our dad. Sometimes—not often, but sometimes—he would agree to let us do something new. It was his way of letting us know he trusted us and that we shouldn't betray that trust.

With all the discipline enforced by both my parents, there was also a lot of hugging and unconditional love in our house.

My husband, who is Greek-Orthodox, was also raised with the belt. Although the belt was rarely used, it made him realize that he should always try to do the right thing—or there would be a serious punishment. He believed the belt would have a positive impact on our children as well, and for this reason he used it a few times. I hated it and cried in the next room when it was being used. Afterwards, I made my husband promise he'd never use the belt again. There is a better way to command respect and make kids listen.

Our kids are being raised with the best of both styles. We believe in the strict ways of our parents, but we also believe that by listening to our children, we are respecting and validating them as individuals. In our discipline efforts, we try to be fair and consistent. At family meetings, we discuss problems and happenings in our kids' lives. We even allow our children to come up with their own consequences for their behavior. Neither my husband nor I had that luxury growing up.

Our children are independent thinkers and express their opinions, but they also understand that there are certain things that are non-negotiable. When they compare our rules with those of their friends', we remind them that for our family, the rules are different—period. For example, going to the movies at night during middle school was unacceptable. They could go in as a group to a matinee, but not at night. At sixteen, our son had to be accompanied by an adult if he was going to the movies at night. He also was not allowed to drive at night. We didn't believe he was ready for those kinds of privileges yet, not because he wasn't mature enough, but because he was still young. Most of his friends were allowed to stay out late, so it had to be hard for him not to. But he accepted the rules. Deep down, he understands that we are strict and protective because that is the way our parents raised us.

At thirteen, our daughter was not allowed to wear certain fashions, and she was expected to call me every hour when she was out with her friends. She was not allowed to go to the mall without an adult, even in the daytime. As for the computer, she was not allowed to have an account with any of the social web pages available for teenagers. There was no dating until she was eighteen. She didn't like that rule, but I remind her that I grew up with the same rule too! If she wanted to date earlier, she had to have a chaperone.

The Latino Versus the American Way of Discipline: Finding a Balance Between the Two Styles of Discipline

Which method works better? Was the way our *abuelas* disciplined us more effective than hearing our kids' side of the story and giving them consequences? Are American parents too lenient? Is it possible to combine a softer touch with a tougher stance? As Latino immigrant parents, we keep a tight rein at home, and we have more rules than our U.S. neighbors. Our kids tend to compare and complain—and sometimes rebel. Some of us may feel that it is inappropriate for kids to question or argue with their parents. We weren't allowed to, so why should they? We may feel that we are losing our authority, especially if our kids were born here, or are better educated than we are, or we don't speak English and they do.

Disciplining our children doesn't have to be a war between them and us—between the American way and the Latino way. Combining the best of both can result in respectful, well-behaved kids. We don't need to feel upset when our children dare to ask us why they can't do something that their friends are allowed to do. They are not necessarily being disrespectful, but are trying to understand our rules. In this country, kids are taught to ask questions—and even to question authority. This doesn't mean we have to agree with them or give in to their

> "Disciplining our children doesn't have to be a war between them and us—between the American way and the Latino way. Combining the best of both can result in respectful, well-behaved kids."

wishes, but we can listen to what they have to say. In fact, if they can learn to articulate their arguments, that is a good thing—even if they don't get their way!

Perhaps instead of dismissing or criticizing the American way of discipline, we can learn to compromise. This means we can accept that it's okay to listen to your child's point of view and talk to them about how your parents disciplined you. Allowing open communication with your children helps them better understand and appreciate their heritage.

The next time your three-year-old child grabs a friend's toy, sit with her and explain that her behavior is not appropriate. Encourage her to say she's sorry to her friend so they can be friends again. It is okay not to spank her. When your ten-year-old refuses to clean his room, sit with him and explain that he is old enough to keep his room clean and that he is expected to do so without complaints. It is okay not to use the belt.

If your kids know the rules from the beginning, they will be more apt to follow them. Children—even teenagers—have to be reminded of the rules often.

My husband has this philosophy about disciplining our kids, which echoes the way our parents raised us: "I am a father, not a friend, and if I have to be unpopular at times, that is okay. Our job as parents is to instill the values we grew up with, the values esteemed by both our Latino and Greek heritages, as well as American culture: respect, hard work, honesty, compassion, kindness, and integrity. But we are also responsible for raising independent, well-rounded individuals. Listening to them is important. Accepting their views is important. Creating a balance between the two cultures, that is the most important. Someday, our children will understand this."

Karina's Story: My Father Disciplined Us the Way He Knew Best

Karina Cabral was born in the U.S.. Her parents are Mexican and came here when they were sixteen years old. They met here, married when they were twenty, and had five children. The family moved back to Mexico when Karina was five and lived there until she was sixteen. Then they immigrated back to the U.S..

Karina's values are strongly rooted in Mexican culture. Her family always speaks Spanish at home, eats Mexican food, and follows Mexican customs. "I had the honor to know what it's like living in poverty," Karina said. "To work on the farm, milking cows, feeding the pigs, and making cheese. But I wanted to get an education."

Her parents agreed to come back to the U.S. to support her dreams. In the small town in Mexico where she grew up, there were no such opportunities. "It wasn't easy for my dad to accept the American value system when we came back. We don't question our parents, and we do as we are told. The kids here don't behave that way. My dad couldn't get used to that."

Karina's dad was the disciplinarian, and he used the belt. "My dad told my older brother and the rest of us not to leave the house while he was gone. Well, my brother didn't listen and left to be with his friends. My siblings and I ran after him to tell him to come back, but all of a sudden we saw my dad. He got so mad he lined us all up and hit us with the belt!" she said.

Her mom disciplined the children differently; she would talk to them and give them consequences, like no television or no outings. "I don't blame my father for the way he disciplined us. Both he and my mother grew up in abusive environments where parents would hit if they got mad at the kids," she said. Karina's mother's parents made her kneel on a bed of ants or made her put her hands flat on the floor and placed rocks on them.

For Karina's parents, it was a shock to witness how much freedom kids had in the States. Girls were allowed to date at a younger age, and teens would go on trips by themselves for a week at time. Students could apply anywhere to go to school, and parents had no problem with that. For Karina's dad, it was hard to accept that she would be leaving home when she was only twenty years old in order to study abroad for a semester. "Girls back home did not do that. They stayed home until they got married," Karina said.

Kids in the States are more independent and tend to be on their own at a younger age. They don't seem to need their parents as much and don't want their parents to tell them what to do. Such freedom and flexibility has made Karina's dad feel less confident about his parenting abilities. "My dad feels like he no longer can prohibit us from doing things because he knows we won't obey him," Karina said. "Back in Mexico, that would not happen. He could tell us what to do, no matter how old we were. He still tries to do things his way, but over the years, he has come to accept many things about the American way."

After she graduated from college, Karina came home from a trip and announced that she had a boyfriend and wanted to marry him. "At first, my dad tried everything he could think of to talk me out of it, but he finally agreed to meet him. That was a major step for him," she said. Today, Karina has a master's degree in the arts of mathematics from the University of Southern California. She is a high school bilingual algebra and geometry teacher, is married to a Costa Rican, and has two children. The couple is raising their children bilingual and bicultural.

As for her father, he still struggles, but he has made peace with Karina's new life. "He has accepted that there are two ways," Karina said. "I keep reminding him that just because I accept my life here doesn't mean I forget where I came from. I belong in both worlds, and I am proud of it."

Success Story: Rodri Rodriguez - Her parents way yielded a renowned entrepreneur, producer and entertainer

Guadalupe Josefina de los Milagros Rodriguez y Rodriguez, Castañeda Laredo, or Rodri Rodriguez, as she has been referred to for the last thirty years, came to the United States alone at age seven. She was part of Operation Peter Pan, an exodus of 14,000 children from Cuba to the United States. Rodri was in a refugee camp for three months before being placed in a foster home for seven years. "I was raised by a family in Albuquerque, and although they were of Mexican heritage, they called themselves Spanish-Americans." This was confusing for Rodri, who at that age didn't know the differences between her culture and her foster family's, and that of her new country. "Confused? This was more like *arroz con mango*," she said.

Discrimination at a young age can be extremely harmful or highly empowering. For Rodri, it was the latter. She recalls being sad most of the time, missing her parents, her home, her surroundings, the ocean, the food, and the customs. Kids would make fun of her Spanish. "But there were also other kids who were ridiculed for being fat or poor. I found myself comforting and defending them. Coming from an island and landing in the middle of the desert was quite traumatic, although the first time I saw and touched snow was amazing and unforgettable," she said.

Rodri's parents were not able to come to America until seven years after her arrival. At fourteen, she felt as if she had to be the parent to her parents, helping them adjust to the States and teaching them the language and cultural differences, including holidays: "For Thanksgiving, my mom would cook the turkey stuffed with picadillo, a very Cuban meat dish, and they would serve black beans and rice with mashed potatoes. It was challenging for them to get used to Christmas being celebrated on the morning of the twenty-fifth since they were used to celebrating Christmas Eve or *La Noche Buena* on the eve of the twenty-fourth, so we did both."

"My parents' adjustment to this country never quite materialized. It was as if we were still in Cuba, but with an ocean only on one side," she said. But it was different for Rodri. "At a young age, I learned to appreciate and embrace the things and people that were different. For me, it was a survival skill. Instead of eating black beans, I learned to enjoy pinto beans. I did not have my parents with me to maintain our traditions, so I learned new ones, took ownership of them, reshaped them a bit, and later, shared them with my parents when they came to America."

Like many immigrant Latino parents, Rodri's parents worked hard during the day and took ESL classes at night. Yet, "they insisted on speaking Spanish and I insisted on speaking English. Quite a battle! I often felt that I was living a double life. This did not change until circumstances forced me to move out," she said.

At age twenty-four, Rodri still had to come home by midnight. One night, she was outside her house discussing symbolism in a Fellini movie with her boyfriend. At 12:30 a.m. she went to the front door, turned the key, and it wouldn't open. Her dad had deadbolted the door. Her mother, who was crying inside the house, told her to go to her brother's house. Rodri slept in her car that night and moved out the next day. "This whole experience was ridiculous. Here I was, the owner of an international company, traveling with major performers to South America and Mexico, but I couldn't miss my dad's curfew or else! This would be more easily digested when one is younger and dependent, but not when one is an adult earning an income. I can still hear my parents when I would ask, 'Why don't you trust me?' and they would answer, 'It is not you we don't trust, it is the outside world,'" she said.

When her parents got older, the roles reversed. Rodri moved her parents into the guest-house on property she purchased. Whenever her mom and dad went out, she required them to tell her where they were going, handed them a curfew, and gave them their own cell phone so she could reach them at any time. Her parents asked, "We are over twenty-one. Why don't you trust us?" and she would reply, "It's not you I don't trust, it is the outside world."

Today, Rodri is a renowned international live concert producer, entrepreneur, entertainer, and founder of MARIACHI USA® Festival, the largest mariachi festival in the world that, since 1990, has played to sold-out audiences at the iconic Hollywood Bowl. Rodri is the founder and chairperson of the MARIACHI USA Foundation, serving more than 5,000 kids over the last eighteen years via scholarships in California, Arizona, Texas, and Washington. "I believe in enriching the lives of youth through the arts, which assisted me in surviving my first seven years in the U.S.. Through the gentle discipline of music and the creative expression of performance, one's-self-esteem can rise from the ashes and triumph over any adversity," she said.

As a child new to this country, Rodri faced discrimination, bullying, and mean-spirited comments on a daily basis from kids her age. "I would be told that my parents did not want me and that they would die when the bombs exploded in Cuba," she said. In her foster home, she survived brutal beatings bordering on torture, with daily emotional and psychological abuse. Rodri held steadfast to the belief that her parents would rescue her one day. She embraced education with a vengeance and won English-language spelling bees, excelled in grammar, and was featured singing in talent shows. "I have much to be thankful for and am living proof that the human spirit can and does overcome," Rodri said.

Rodri's story is one of survival, hope, acceptance, courage, and love. It reflects what children feel when they are first separated from their parents to come to this country

> "I believe in enriching the lives of youth through the arts, which assisted me in surviving my first seven years in the U.S."

and how hard the adjustment can be. My hope is that when parents read this, they can better understand what some of their children go through when they first come here. I also hope that parents will understand how important it is to talk, listen, and take time to help the children adjust to their new life.

Tips for Latino Immigrant Parents on the Balance Between Two Styles of Discipline

Here are my parenting tips to help you balance the two styles of disciplining your children: the Latino way and the American way.

1. Accept that you are raising your kids in a different world from the one in which you grew up. It's not necessarily better or worse—just different.

2. With your spouse, establish rules for your children's behavior that are clear, concise and consistent. Establish consequences for when they disobey.

3. Sit down with your kids and discuss the rules and consequences with them. Explain why your rules are important and why they are expected to honor them. Also tell them that you are willing to compromise on certain rules, but not on others.

4. Listen to your child's point of view, thereby demonstrating your respect for him as an individual. When you do this, your

children will actually have more respect for you.

5.   Give your child a chance to express his opinion, but let them know that you are the authority and have final say.

6.   If you feel like you are losing ground with your kids, stop and really listen to what they have to say. Then, give them a chance to listen to you.

7.   Establish monthly family meetings to discuss how the balancing of two ways of discipline is working out for the family.

My Parenting Journal

Write down the thoughts and feelings that came to mind while you read this chapter. Here are some topics that might help you get started:

1.   Have you accepted that you can raise your kids with two disciplinary styles?

2.   Do you see the benefits of using both the American way and the Latino way of disciplining your children? Why? Why not?

3.   If you have not found a balance between the two ways of disciplining your kids, how is that affecting them?

4.   Sit down and make a list of the differences you notice between the ways your parents disciplined you and the ways children are disciplined in America.

5.   With the list in hand, discuss with your spouse which privileges or behaviors you are willing to compromise on and which are non-negotiable. For example, children here are allowed to have sleepovers at their friends' houses. Would you allow your kids to do that? At what age would they be allowed to do that? Would that be a negotiable rule or a non-negotiable rule?

6.   Write down the final draft of the list of rules and consequences that you have compiled with the input of your

spouse and children. Have the entire family sign and date the list, and post it on your refrigerator or another easily accessible and visible location. If you write them down, and everyone takes ownership, children are more likely to comply. When, and if necessary, update the list.

Chapter 7: Special Concerns for the Single Immigrant Parent

"After ten years of marriage and three children, my husband left me. I had nothing. I came to America to find a better life for my children. It has been a hard adjustment for all of us."
—Ana, age 35

As a married mother of two children, I can only imagine what it would be like to raise my son and daughter by myself. Parenting is not an easy job. It is hard work and it never ends—no matter how old your children are. Single parents face greater challenges. What happens when mom is sick or tired or angry? She can't walk away and let a spouse take over. What happens if she has two jobs and no family around to help with the kids? She will have to learn to trust someone. And what happens if she and the father of their children share custody, but can't find common ground when necessary? How are the kids affected by the lack of compassion parents show each other and their constant arguments? And what if we become a teenage mom? That makes life even more complicated. Psychologist and author, Dr. Ana Nogales, believes that Latinas are raised to be mothers. "We are taught babies are a blessing and we ought to want many of them. A baby loves us and it gives us a sense of belonging. Perhaps that is why many Latina girls get pregnant, to have someone who loves them unconditionally. With education, communication, and self-confidence, we can break that stereotype," she said.

The following stories highlight many of the issues with which single parents in the immigrant community must grapple. As you read them, you will be able to relate to some aspect of what each of these parents went through—and be encouraged by how others in your situation coped with the stresses of single parenting.

Isabel's Story: My Kids Were Influenced by Their Americanized Friends

Isabel never thought about how her kids' behavior might change as a result of their desire to fit in with their friends. Nor did she consider how her style of parenting might change when she moved to the U.S. from El Salvador. Her goal was to simply bring up her kids safely and with more opportunities. She had come to the U.S. by herself five years before while her kids stayed behind with relatives. When they arrived, Isabel's oldest son was a teenager, her daughter a preteen, and her youngest was eight. She figured that since she adapted well to her new life, her kids wouldn't have any problems either.

It wasn't until her eight-year-old stopped talking and the older kids stopped following the rules, that Isabel realized something was missing. She had been a long-distance mom for five years. Now, her kids were reunited with her, and she was trying to parent the only way she knew how—the way her parents did it. There were strict rules about curfew, clothes, how to behave with adults, and how to contribute with chores. Her kids' friends didn't have so many rules, and Isabel's kids began to rebel.

Isabel had thought her kids were adjusting well to life in America. "Perhaps too well," she said. "All of the sudden, I started noticing that they were not following the rules." Isabel's oldest son, Mario, did not want to speak Spanish at all. He would constantly fight with her about curfew and didn't want his mom to meet his new friends. In his quest to belong, Mario befriended kids who wore dark clothes, had pierced noses, and didn't care much about school. Isabel was so tired from working two jobs that sometimes she didn't even want to discuss what was going on with her oldest son.

Her eight-year-old felt self-conscious about not being able to speak English. His mother made him dress conservatively, unlike the kids at school, who wore jeans and t-shirts. Feeling insecure and left-out, he began to misbehave.

Both boys would say, "I don't have to listen to you, Mami," or "I am not going to do that—it's too much work." They would lie about finishing their homework or where they were after school.

Frustrated, Isabel opted to neglect her parental responsibilities: "I was the only one in charge. It was easier to bend the rules and ignore a behavior that I would have never accepted back home, like sleeping over at a friend's whom I had never met." Isabel had mistakenly assumed that her kids were proud of their heritage and would not question the values they had grown up with. "I thought they would know what was acceptable and what wasn't, that they would behave according to the ways I had taught them, even while adjusting to how it is here," she said.

The kids were constantly arguing with her and among themselves. She finally decided to go to her church and talk to her priest about her situation. Her priest introduced her to other immigrant parents who had gone through similar experiences.

Speaking with these parents, Isabel learned to better deal with her children's problems. She brought them to church every Sunday where they made friends who were also immigrants and spoke Spanish. The church had a program for immigrant children with a psychologist who listened to the children's concerns. Isabel's kids were able to talk about their experiences, and they realized that everyone they met had a hard time adjusting, but that it could be done. It helped that their new friends and the psychologist spoke in Spanish. They learned other kids took English classes after school every day for months until they were able to measure up to the kids in their grade.

Isabel learned she could instill the old values while accepting many of the new ones. For example, she learned it was okay to allow her children to wear less conservative clothes, like board shorts for the boys and jeans for her daughter. There was also more communication between her and her children—something valued in the U.S., but perhaps not so much in El Salvador. Most importantly, Isabel learned to ask for and to accept help. "Knowing that I could count on others helped me become a better parent," she said.

Irma's Story: Choosing to Be a Single Parent

Irma was twenty-two and unmarried when she moved to the States from Puerto Vallarta, Mexico. She moved in with her cousin, who lived in a neighborhood where there were few Latinos. When they wanted to be around people from their culture, they had to drive an hour to a different neighborhood. Irma was so homesick, she was tempted to return to Mexico. "That first year was the worst," she said. "I had one foot here and the other back home." She worked as a housekeeper. Even though her family in Mexico was not rich, they were not poor, and she had studied for a technical career and briefly worked as a secretary. "Working as a housekeeper was humiliating for me, although my employers were nice people. I think feeling lonely made the situation even worse," she said. She didn't have many friends and only saw her cousin on the weekend. Her cousin was supportive and understanding as she too, had had to adjust to a new life. Then the rest of her family joined her in Los Angeles, and life became less isolated.

"I had some pretty rough times. I was homesick all the time, I didn't like my job, my cousin was an hour away, I had no friends, I was lonely and sad most of the time, but that experience helped me become a strong and independent woman," she said.

Then she got pregnant. She was twenty-five years old and didn't marry the father of her child because he was already married.

She made the choice of raising her baby alone: "When I decided to have my baby, I really didn't know what I was going to do or what I was getting into. I was young and inexperienced and thought I was invincible. I could do everything! I could raise a child alone. But over the years, I felt guilty that I made the choice of not including her father in my daughter's life. I was angry at his betrayal and at his reaction towards my pregnancy, but I didn't think of how important it is for a child to have a mother and a father. She had the right to know her father; I understand that now."

Irma's daughter, Vanessa, is eleven years old, in sixth grade, and bilingual. Although she has no contact with her father, Vanessa is a happy child. Irma's brothers are the masculine role models in her daughter's life. "I think at times, not to having a dad affects her," Irma says. "She has been raised without him, and I think she resents that, especially when she sees that her friends have dads." Irma asked Vanessa if she wants to meet her father and tried to explain why he wasn't part of their lives. Vanessa is not interested.

> "Knowing that I could count on others helped me become a better parent."

Irma believes that having survived the adjustment to this country in those early years helped her raise her daughter alone: "Physically and emotionally, I was alone. I had to learn to be alone and to appreciate how my life changed when I moved to this country. I had to learn to be independent and to trust my decisions." Once her family came, they became her greatest strength since her daughter was born. Her mother and siblings have given her advice, support, love, and encouragement. She has taken parenting classes and read many parenting books. "It is a challenge to be a single mother. I sometimes long for a partner, but after three or four attempts over the last few years, I decided that I have had enough. Right now I am focusing on my career and guiding Vanessa through the challenging teenage years. I am both the permissive and the strict parent, the good and the bad, the ugly and the pretty, the mother and the father. Easy? Not at all, but I have done it so far. I am proud of my accomplishment," she said.

To Irma, one of the main differences between the way she was raised and the way her daughter is being raised is the open communication. She talks to her daughter all the time. Irma's mother did not talk to her much. "We were told what do to, not why we had to do it," she said. Growing up, she was daddy's little girl, but her father left the family when she was nineteen years old. "Although I grew up with a dad until I was a teenager, I do understand what it is like not to have one around. That helps me when raising my daughter. I can relate to how she feels," she said. When her daughter misbehaves, Irma takes privileges away rather than hitting her, which is how Irma was raised. On the other hand, Irma sees there were benefits to the Latino parenting style: "Children respected more and complained less. They had better manners when I was growing up. Now, they take things for granted, and they expect things right now! They are not being raised to be grateful, nor to respect authority." Her daughter knows that at her house, things are different. She can't get away with tantrums, she has to respect her elders, and follow the house rules. "She does well in school, and she is proud of her two cultures, especially now that we have visited Mexico. That is very important to me."

Lupita's Story: A Teenage Mom Who Was Never Mothered Herself

Lupita was born in Guadalajara, Mexico. She came to the U.S. when she was fourteen and already the mother of a one-year-old boy, Jaime. Her story is filled with pain, betrayal, loneliness, and, finally, forgiveness.

Lupita had a tough childhood. Her mother, Mayra, left her and her brother with her grandmother when Lupita was a baby. Like countless other immigrants, Mayra came to the States in search of a better life. Lupita was five years old before she would see her mother again. "My grandmother had twelve kids, plus the two of us to take care of. I didn't have a fun, loving, caring mother to watch over me. My grandma did her best and she taught me good values, but there were too many of us for her to devote time to each one," she said. Lupita never knew her father, so her father figure was her grandfather: "My grandfather and I had a special bond. He taught me how to raise hens and how to take care of our horses and the other animals in the old ranch we lived on." Her grandfather did his best to help her live without a mother and father. "But I was always dreaming of my mom. I missed her, especially at bedtime. She was not there to read me a book or tuck me in. I had no place to go if I was scared during the night. My mom was not there," she said.

Lupita got pregnant at thirteen and came to the U.S., partly in search of her mother and partly because she thought she would marry the father of her child. Instead, they broke up and she never saw him again. Barely a teenager and already a mother, Lupita felt lost and abandoned all over again. At fourteen, she had seen her mom for only the second time in her life, and the relationship was filled with resentment.

Her early years in the U.S. were "like a nightmare," she said. Not only was she adjusting to a new life, she was a new mother and trying to help her son adapt. During the year or so that she lived with her mother, Lupita went to high school and learned English, but the relationship between mother and daughter wasn't working. "We didn't know each other," Lupita said. "There were many problems, such as lack of trust and lack of emotional connection." Eventually, Lupita and her son ended up in the foster care system.

Lupita went to school and also worked while a foster mother took care of her baby son. Although the foster father was a nice man and treated Lupita and her son kindly, the foster mother routinely spanked Jaime. It wasn't until her son spoke to a therapist who was assigned to their case that he and Lupita were able to leave the abusive foster home. Unfortunately, this meant that Lupita had to transfer out of the school she'd been attending. Since she was forced to switch schools, Lupita had to attend high school for another year and a half before she was able to graduate. She felt discouraged about having to endure one more detour on the path she was trying to carve out for herself. Also, she and her son ended up in a group home, "which was even harder for my son," she said. She kept trying to stay positive.

Lupita knew that the only way she was going to give her son a better life was to become educated. She wanted more for her son than what she had as a child. But in some ways, she was neglecting him in order to further her education. She was lucky to find help from her group home roommates, but her son wanted her and needed her. "The whole time I was finishing school, my focus was on becoming a better mother than my mother had been to me. I wanted to be a good example for him." Lupita said.

After a while, Lupita was able to move to a center that assisted unwed pregnant young women, as well as unwed young mothers and their children who had been released from the child welfare system.

Today Lupita is going to college. "My son still struggles, but now we have a home and we spend more time together, and I have learned so much more about parenting," Lupita said. She also has a better relationship with her own mother. "I understand now that my mother came here following the American dream. She wanted a better life for all of us. When she left, I was too young and resented her leaving. I missed her and was hurt that she chose to leave us. Now that I am older and I am a mother, I see why she made that choice."

> "My son still struggles, but now we have a home and we spend more time together, and I have learned so much more about parenting."

Lupita wants her son to appreciate his Latino heritage and his American life. "I want him to know he can dream and he can achieve, but he should never forget where he came from," she said.

Rita's Story: Overcoming Culture Shock, Deportation, Divorce, and Sexism

Rita was eleven, the product of a broken home, when she came to the U.S.. Her mother, Carmen, had divorced Rita's father and left her and her sisters with a cousin. A year and a half later, Rita joined her mother in the U.S..

It took Rita a long time to adjust. She not only had to get used to a new culture, she also had to adjust to a downturn in her family's socio-economic status. Rita came from an upper middle class background in Mexico City. Growing up, she had everything a girl of her stature could want: attractive and successful parents, a beautiful house, maids who catered to her every need, and secure standing in a local private school. When her parents divorced, she lost all of that. Her parents had dual custody of her and her siblings, but her dad disappeared from their lives and her mother had to work to support the family.

Carmen worked as a high fashion seamstress, but was looked down on by her former friends now that she was part of the working class. In those days, she was considered tainted, due to her status as a divorced woman. Her ex-friends gossiped about her, making up stories about why she was a threat to their husbands. Although Rita's father had had another wife and children while married to her mother; Carmen was the one who was looked down upon.

A woman who had been one of Carmen's clients helped her start a sewing business in the U.S.. When the girls joined her, they all had to pitch in sewing the clothes. It was a totally different life than the one they had in Mexico. Rita and her sisters didn't speak English, and when they went to school, they felt like outcasts, even though they dressed better than the other children and were better educated.

For a long time, Rita and her sisters were bullied by the other kids. They didn't retaliate because, in Mexico, they were taught that young ladies don't fight. For many months, they took the abuse and didn't tell anyone about it. "During that period, I learned survival skills that have helped me throughout my life," Rita said. "It used to take me two hours to get home because I took a route where the bullies couldn't find me." One day, one of Rita's sisters had enough. "She broke the bully's leg. That was the last time we were bullied!"

Around the same time, Rita's mother and stepfather were taken by immigration officials. She and her sisters waited all night without any news. Finally, they received a phone call and found out that their mother and stepfather were in Tijuana. It took them ten days to cross back to the U.S. In the meantime, Rita, being the oldest at eleven, organized and ran the household, designed a budget, and paid the bills. "That week I thought about what I needed to do with the rest of my life. I actually planned what my life would look like up through the age of thirty. I didn't include college. It took me longer to get there."

Rita learned English very quickly, but she wasn't happy. She felt as if she couldn't trust anyone. First her father had led a double life and abandoned her and her siblings, then her mother left for another country, then Rita had to adjust to the U.S. where she was bullied. As a result, she became a loner: "It was better to be alone than to try to make friends with those kids I had nothing in common with. And I was afraid of getting close."

Rita was especially resentful of her father. After he left, she and her sisters had no contact with him. Then one day, they saw him—he turned the other way and didn't even acknowledged them. Years later, when her sister needed him to sign some papers in order for her to come to the U.S. legally, he wouldn't sign them, and her sister had to come into the country with no documents. Rita never saw her father again and has never forgiven him. "If I had a real father, a loving, caring dad, my life would have been different. Instead, so many things happened because he was not around," she said. While growing up in Tijuana without her father, she and her two sisters were molested by a cousin's husband. "It took me twelve years before I could talk about what happened."

Unfortunately, Rita ended up marrying a man who was as emotionally abusive as her father had been. The marriage produced two children. "Because of what happened to me as a child, I never trusted any man. I never left my children alone with my husband, yet I stayed married to him for twenty-two years because I was convinced they needed a father. I didn't want them to be as affected by not having a father as I had been," she said. Rita used to believe that children needed both a father and a mother; she has since learned that what children need is quality parenting.

"As a father, Miguel was fun. He loved to tease the kids, and he kept everything light-hearted. However, he never disciplined nor helped with homework. If he ever took the kids to their extracurricular activities, he would complain the whole time," she said

Rita still remembers how her son would beg his dad to help with homework and how his daughter would plead for a dollhouse. "He never helped and he never built it," she said.

Still, when Rita announced that she and her husband were getting a divorce, her daughter was angry at her and her son was terribly hurt. "My husband had me convinced that I was a bad parent because of my job and my traveling. Yet, he loved the perks and the prestige of my position. I was supposed to be a stay-at-home mom, but he encouraged me to work and I was more successful at my job than he was. I was everything a traditional mother was; my only sin was that I worked too," she said.

Rita is convinced that all of her difficult experiences have contributed to the person and the mother she is today: "I have spent many years creating walls around me and my kids, so that we do not get hurt. I have only a handful of people I trust and consider my friends. No one can or will take care of me, or my kids, and I will have to figure out how to get them what they need. Asking for financial support of any sort is extremely difficult, and I would rather go hungry than ask."

Today, Rita's kids live with her, and they don't want to talk to their dad. They are older now and understand the pain their mother endured in the marriage and why she decided to file for divorce. Her son has even written about his family's experience in English class, telling everyone what a great mom he has.

> "We are all capable of overcoming even the most heart wrenching experiences if we put our minds to it and have the *ganas* (desire) to. Even a single mom."

"I was lucky enough to have wonderful people help me and mentor me along the way," Rita said. "My first boss when I was seventeen taught me to believe in myself, and he challenged me. I took his advice, and I am where I am today partly because of what he taught me. I want that for my kids. I want them to believe in themselves, to trust themselves, and to always look ahead with their head held high. They have the best of two worlds, and I want them to take advantage of that, like I have."

Like Rita, a good single parent puts herself first before her children and strives to be a good example regardless of the struggles and moves ahead instead of dwelling on the circumstances. "We are all capable of overcoming even the most heart wrenching experiences if we put our minds to it and have the *ganas* (desire) to. Even a single mom," she said.

Meeting the Challenges of Single Parenthood

It is not impossible to raise children alone successfully. Admitting that it is hard is the first step, while the second step is to acknowledge that you need help and not be afraid to ask for it. Perhaps your best friend can help with your children. Couldn't the two of you work out a plan to help each other with childcare and emergencies? What about your neighbor down the street or the woman who works with you in the office or at the hotel or factory? Might one of these women appreciate the opportunity to trade babysitting nights with you or to be there for you—and you for her—when one of you needs help with a sick child? Perhaps the lady you met at the park might be looking for help with her children, and the two of you could trade off taking the kids to the playground on your days off.

Your church is also a good place to look for childcare help. For example, St. Lawrence Brindisi in South Central Los Angeles has about 3,000 families registered, 90 percent of which are Latino. The staff and volunteers are from all walks of life. From ESL classes to an information center, to an advocacy referral program for social, medical, and legal problems to an amazing youth center, St. Lawrence is there to help the community. Formerly led by Father Peter Banks, who was totally dedicated to the people in the neighborhood—the families of this parish and the homeless on the street—the Parish, now led by Father Jesús, is not just a church for their spiritual needs, but a social center for them to gather for friendship and support.

Most likely, your church or local community center has free recreational programs that would be a good way for your kids to meet other children, as well as a male authority figure with whom they might identify with. It is very important to recognize that our children need the attention and involvement of a caring male role model. Whether it's a grandfather, uncle, older cousin, or a male friend of yours, their consistent involvement will strengthen your child's feeling of being loved and cared for. If your children's father has left home or is never around, this is especially important.

"Fathers are important in a child's life for a number of reasons," said Dr. Nogales. "First of all, a father symbolizes protection and security. For girls, growing up without a father can result in an idealization of what a father is supposed to be. As she gets older, the lack of a father or male figure can have a significant impact on her relationship with men. She can become clingy, avoidant, or have a hard time bonding." For boys, Nogales believes that not having a father around can result in difficult behavior. "A father is an important role model for the way we act. When there is no father around, it is imperative to find a male adult that can fulfill the role of a father." Marriage and family therapist Mary Klem added, "Our sense of self is developed through our relationship with mom and dad. When there is no dad figure, there is a sense of abandonment, a lack of attachment, no sense of identity, and no grounding. Children need that reinforcement, that reflection from their main attachment figures."

Your children's teachers are also good resources. You need to know what's going on at school, and your child's teachers need to know what is happening at home, so that your child receives the attention he requires. For instance, if a teacher is informed that there has been a divorce or separation in your family, the teacher will know to be aware of any emotional or behavioral changes in your child. Your child's teacher may also be able to tell you how your child is feeling about the divorce or the separation, and may offer suggestions as to how to handle things at home. Perhaps a school counselor can help in this regard. If you do not speak English well and your child's teacher doesn't speak Spanish well, ask a friend to translate.

One single mom with four children, one of whom has a serious medical condition, had a caring neighbor who was a consistent presence in this woman's home—helping with a load of laundry, a meal, or a crying baby. A divorced couple I know has been able to let go of the hurt and now put their children's welfare first by and helping each other out. The kids are with their mother for half the week and with the father for the other half and every other weekend. This allows both of them to have breaks, and helps the children develop and nurture relationships with both parents.

The point is to realize that there is help out there. If you are raising your children without a father, you need to acknowledge that you need that help - and then do whatever you can to get it. Sometimes all you have to do is ask.

Deborah Castillero's Story: A Father's Support of Culture Can Make a Difference

Deborah was born in the United States and grew up in Rochester, New York. Her dad is Caucasian, and her mom is from Panamá. When she was seven years old, Deborah's mom sent her to her grandmother in Panamá. She spent that summer in the rural town of Guararé. "I went down there as a little gringa who spoke no Spanish and came back a gringa-Latina who spoke Spanish fluently and fell in love with her culture," she said.

Although Deborah grew up in the States, she was raised bicultural. Her mom comes from a large family, and every weekend, the family would gather, speaking lots of Spanish, eating Latino food, and playing Spanish music in the background. Through her mother's work for the Rochester City School District, Deborah was also exposed to many Hispanic cultural and educational events. "Being exposed to Spanish and my Latino culture at a young age helped me identify with my heritage. Those experiences have shaped who I am as a woman, daughter, and friend," she said.

There is also her role as a single mom. Her son, now an adult, grew up with two cultures, American and Panamanian. "There were multiple trips to Panama that helped us stay connected to the culture. Being bicultural means I get to live in two beautiful cultures, an experience I find quite enriching. I wanted to ensure my son had the same kind of wonderful experience," she said.

From an early age, Deborah and her son spent every summer in Panama with the family, so he was exposed to the language and culture.

Latin music was played at home, and she would take him to Latino-centric cultural festivals, just as her mother did with her. "Latino cuisine is probably his favorite of all the culinary delights. Speaking Spanish was also a priority, and we always had a Spanish-speaking *Ama de Casa* (housekeeper) at home to reinforce his second language speaking skills," she said.

Through the years, Deborah appreciated her ex-husband's support for the dual language and bicultural life: "My son's dad loves the Latino culture and was very supportive of our son learning a second language and connecting to his heritage."

When asked if it was difficult to balance both cultures at home, she said, "I never found this to be a chore, but more a natural expression of my affinity towards my heritage. In our home, there were two ways to say one things: in English and in Spanish."

Today, Deborah is a self-proclaimed *gringa-Latina* who always straddles two cultures. She's the founder and CEO of Tipi Tom Tales, a startup focused on exposing preschoolers to a second language.

Tips for Latino Single Parents

1. Acknowledge that raising your children alone means you need help.
2. Accept that it is okay to ask for help.
3. Visit your nearby church and/or library, and talk to the activities director to find out what type of programs they offer for children and families. Sign up!
4. Visit your local community center and find out about recreational programs for the kids. Sign them up!
5. Talk to your children on an ongoing basis—and listen to what they have to say.
6. Find out how they feel about friends, school, home life, and living within two cultures. Don't be afraid to bring up the subject of their not having a dad, if that is the case, or about living between two homes, if that is the situation. The

important thing is to have an open line of communication and to allow your children to express their feelings.

7. Be honest and be human. It is okay for your children to know that you are tired, and it is also okay if you occasionally lose your temper. If you have been overly harsh with them, at the end of the day, when you tuck them in, tell them that you are sorry you lost your temper—and that you love them.

8. Tell your kids you love them ALL THE TIME! But stay firm and consistent in your enforcement of the rules, even though this can be more difficult as a single parent. Kids need love, but they also need rules and structure.

9. Encourage a relationship between your child and his father, especially if you don't have a good relationship with him yourself. Try to show respect toward your child's father, even if you don't feel like it. Not only will it mean a lot to your child that you are courteous to his father, you will also be setting a good example on how to treat people politely and behave maturely.

My Parenting Journal

Raising children alone is a big responsibility. Making that choice is not easy and it can be overwhelming. Understand that you are not alone and that you don't have to do this alone. As you reflect upon the stories you just read and ponder their similarities to yours, write down your feelings and concerns. Here are some suggestions to get you started.

1. Am I being the best parent I can be?
2. Do I feel overwhelmed at times and in need of assistance?
3. Do I take the time to look for help and accept what others have to offer?
4. If not, write a list of appropriate people whom you trust and could ask for help. Consider relatives, neighbors, friends, co-workers, and church members.

5. Am I finding opportunities for my children to interact with other children who are in similar situations, so they can understand they are not alone?

6. Is there a male role model in my children's life?

7. If not, why not and how can I change that?

8. Do I find time for myself? Do I find time to do something for me?

9. Do I look at my life and try to teach my kids to do better and better?

Chapter 8: Home Sweet Home: The Pros and Cons of Going Back Home

"I love going back home to visit. But after all these years in America, I have mixed feelings about going back…I wouldn't want to live there again."
—Magali, age 56

Going back home to visit is a luxury for most. Yet, I think it is important to discuss how we feel about going back to our country of origin. Depending on the circumstances, we end up going back to visit our family because we want to, we have to, or because it is the right thing to do. Oftentimes, we really want to go home, but we can't. We don't have papers, don't have the time, or are afraid to cross the border when we might not be able to make it back again. For some people, going back is too expensive and it may take years before they are able to go. As parents, we have to raise our kids with the idea that they might be going back to visit, and, that if such a trip happens, they should feel excited and grateful about it. After all, life as they know it here is not the same as life is going to be back there. Our kids need to understand that and appreciate the differences. Kids learn by example. If we are excited about going back home to visit our family, they will grow up being excited about it, too. It is up to us to teach them about the differences, similarities, and about how to deal with both.

"I remember the excitement of going back home, feeling that my stay in the United States was not definite and that home was still where I was born," says Dr. Ana Nogales. "Believing I was really returning home, I wanted to take my shoes off as soon as I boarded the plane and just hold on to the idea that I really was going home for good!"

According to Nogales, this is a common feeling among immigrants who are born in geographical areas closer to the U.S., as they can go back and forth more often than others. However, as time goes by and immigrants establish new bonds, home starts to change location and becomes the place you live, where you raise your children and work, where you wake up every morning for coffee, and where you go back to bed after a day of work. Home becomes where you establish yourself, not where you were born anymore. "In the meantime, many things happen to make you feel that way," says Nogales, "and more than not, it likely is a life event process, as most never totally disconnect from their roots."

> "You may have conflicts deciding which place is home and feelings of loyalty for one place or another, or perhaps feelings of betrayal for one place if the other becomes more prominent in your mind."

The adjustment is not easy. You may have conflicts deciding which place is home and feelings of loyalty for one place or another, or perhaps feelings of betrayal for one place if the other becomes more prominent in your mind.

The first six months in a new country are like a honeymoon for the immigrant, and then reality starts to set in, and people start to miss home more. Unfortunately, many immigrants are not able to return home, and that contributes to the idealization that what we left behind was better than what we found here. Some people go back after ten or twenty years, and they become disappointed because their memories are not the same as the new reality.

My friend Cecilia admits that what she missed the most was her family, especially her mom and her childhood friends: "That kind of friendship, it survives distance and time." Yet, when asked if she would go back to Argentina, where she emigrated from, Cecilia said, "No, our life is here in the States. We have a better life, a more comfortable life. But we will always go visit." Cecilia believes that the best thing that has happened to help immigrants find a balance is the new technology: "Facebook and Skype allow me to be in contact with my family and friends more often and without effort. Now I can sit down with my sister, and we both enjoy a cup of coffee or cook together—but she is there and I am here!"

Yulisa was in high school when she came to the United States from the Dominican Republic. She went back for the first time almost three years later. "It was so hard to leave all my childhood and high school friends behind," she said. Yulisa brings back coffee and a heart full of love and memories. "I can't explain the feeling, but I just come back filled with love and am happy to be alive. Being surrounded by my people has that effect on me and I treasure it." She said that she would like to be back one day. "There is nothing like our people, our food, and our culture. Yes, someday, I will be back for good."

The next three stories are examples of how some of us have dealt with going back to our native country, and how we have found the balance with two cultures in our new home. Perhaps they remind you of your own story.

Kela's Story: Going Back to Visit is a Tradition

Kela came here from El Salvador in 1983. She came escaping the war. She had lost her husband and her house. Her husband was captured by the *guerrilleros*, and her house was burned down. She lost everything she owned and would have lost her life and that of her ten-month-old baby if she had not left her house before the soldiers barged in. The decision to leave her country was hard, but since her sister was already in the States, Kela decided she was going to follow her and try and make a better life for herself and her daughter. But, like many others before her, she had to leave her baby behind. Her parents took care of the baby when Kela crossed the border and began her new life. "It took ten years before I went back to visit," said Kela. "By then, the war was over and my family had immigrated to a smaller town nearby. They too lost everything they owned during the war." Kela still remembers those first few moments when the airplane landed in San Salvador. "I will never forget the view from the airplane. I was finally in my country again, my beautiful country," she said. "The emotions were overwhelming, I was so happy." But her return was also bittersweet. "It brought back all those memories of what I had left behind and why. To this day, my then-husband has never been found."

After that first visit and once the war was over, it was a lot easier for Kela to go back to her country. Her work permit allowed her to travel freely. "The hardest part was leaving my daughter Carla behind," said Kela. "She was three years old the first time I saw her after I fled. She came to live with me, but that didn't work out. I was busy working to make money and trying to adjust to this country; I couldn't take care of her." After two years, Carla went back to El Salvador when she was five years old. She would only see her mom once a year until she was seventeen years old and came to live in the United States for good.

At seventeen, Carla had a hard time adjusting to her new life in the United States. She didn't speak English, and she really didn't know her mother. Plus, she now had three younger sisters to learn to live with. And her sisters were American. She felt rejected and cried all the time. Kela tried to help her and was supportive of her efforts, but it took Carla a long time to find a balance and feel at home. Her boyfriend from El Salvador came after her, and they got pregnant at eighteen. They moved to San Francisco and then to Denver where Carla finished college. She and her boyfriend got married and have two children. "Our relationship is better now," said Kela. "We are more like friends than a mother-daughter. At least it is something."

"My girls have all grown up with two cultures," said Kela, "Even Carla. All those years I went to see her, I took her sisters with me. I wanted them all to be a family. I wanted my American-born girls to appreciate their roots and their heritage. It was important for my husband and I. He is also from El Salvador, and we met in the United States. Both of us fled the horrible conditions there in the early '80s." Kela's second husband and father of her three younger daughters is also the adoptive father of Carla. "He loves her like a father, and tries to help her adjust."

Kela loves to bring back food from El Salvador. Her favorite is *Pan Dulce* (sweet breads), cheeses, and creams. "It all tastes better when it is from there," she said. She also brings back *artesanias* (art crafts). "Everything there is handmade; it is just all so beautiful."

For seven years now, Kela has gone back once a year to visit with her siblings. "In my country, we have a tradition. When a parent dies, we go back every year to reunite with family and to honor the deceased. It gives us a chance to stay close to our roots," said Kela.

Candida's Story: Dreams of Going Back for Good

Candida has been in the United States for eighteen years. Like Kela, it took her ten years to go back and visit her country of Nicaragua. "It was always in my mind to go back and visit," said Candida. To her, not going to visit for that long had an emotional impact. "All of the sudden, we are so enthralled with our life here, it is easy to feel like we are more from here than from there. But one is always longing for our old life."

Family and friends are what Candida missed most from her life in Nicaragua. She also misses the sunsets: "I can't explain it. The sky is bluer and the sun setting against it, it is just magical."

Candida's adjustment to her new life was a positive one. Learning English was difficult, but she was determined. She mostly learned it on the job. She has worked with families in the same neighborhood since the beginning, and has raised many of their children. "Some of the kids are now young adults. They were babies when I started. It has been a rewarding experience. I have met a lot of kindness here," she said.

When Candida left Nicaragua, her oldest son, Luis, stayed behind. He was only six years old. He joined her when he was a teenager. "He was resentful and didn't like me very much for a long time," Candida said. "It was hard for him to understand why I left." When asked how she managed to salvage her relationship with Luis, she said, "I actually asked him for forgiveness. I explained the why of the circumstances. He was older then, and he was able to understand and to forgive." Luis went to high school in the States and then went back to Nicaragua for a few years before settling back in the States. Candida got remarried and has another son, Geanly, born in this country. "I have raised my

121

two sons with two cultures. Their lives have been enriched by growing up appreciating their heritage and the vast opportunities America has offered them," she said. Where she comes from, they are proud of the fact that they have family in the States. "Coming to America to find a better life, it is a dream for my people in Nicaragua. When one does it, it is considered an accomplishment. We are here now, but one day, one day, we will go back there for good," she said.

My Story: California is Home

I was twenty-one years old when I left Puerto Rico. I went to California to attend college. It was never my intention nor was it my interest to stay there. I was going to study, finish, then pack my bags and go back HOME! Fortunately, life had other plans for me. I ended up falling in love, and after getting married in my hometown of Ponce in Puerto Rico, I was back in California permanently. My husband and I have made a life here and almost thirty years later, I call Los Angeles home. I am one of the lucky ones that get to visit Puerto Rico often. When my children were little, I would go in the summer. The last few years we have been going during the Christmas holidays. It really is a fun time to go visit family and enjoy all the traditional foods and activities. The whole island is on vacation over the holidays and it is one big party after another.

What I love the most is that it is all about family and close friends. It is the time to reconnect and honor our traditions: the food, the gatherings, the activities—they all honor the real meaning of Christmas. There, it all seems more spiritual and more solemn. Oh, they party, and the noise level is grandiose, the laughs are boisterous, and everyone is on high spirits and happy. Although the atmosphere is on a high, the mood is always on holy ground. At least, it is what I feel when I am there. There is a big emphasis on *Las Misas de Aguinaldo*, the traditional 5:00 a.m. masses that are held in most Catholic churches from December 15 to December 23. Christmas Eve is a big family event, as is mass on Christmas Day and family again after. It is our Puerto Rican way of honoring family, extended family, and close friends.

During the holidays on the island, we eat a lot of pork, as in roasted pig, *arroz con gandules* (rice with pigeon peas), and *pasteles*, made with mashed soft green plantains and stuffed with olives, chicken, or pork. We also eat *mofongo* (this we eat all the time there), a dough-like mixture made with soft green plantains, garlic, and bacon bits, among other ways. The one stuffed with seafood is a favorite of my husband. While we are there visiting, my mom makes all the food that I grew up with, and that have become staples in my own home: *arroz con pollo* (rice with chicken), *habichuelas* (red and pinto beans), *lomo encebollado*, (meat with onions), and my favorite, *carne mechada* (roast rump stuffed with olives and ham). My family's favorite? Abi's (that is what my children called my mother) shrimp and garlic with *arroz blanco* (white rice).

> "After being there a few weeks, I feel recharged by the love of family and close childhood friends and am ready to go home."

After being there a few weeks, I feel recharged by the love of family and close childhood friends and am ready to go home. Yet, there is always a nostalgic feeling when the plane takes off from San Juan, especially now that my parents are older. California is home now and that won't change, but we will always go back to visit. It is a family tradition.

Tips for Latino Parents on the Pros and Cons of Going Back Home

There are pros and cons about going back home to visit. The following questions can help you understand your feelings about visiting your homeland.

1. Accept that it might take years before you are able to go back to visit.
2. If money is the hurdle you need to get over, start saving,

even if it is only a small amount at a time. Small amounts add up.

3. While planning your trip home, be open to feeling a wide range of emotions. You may feel everything from regret and fear to joy and nostalgia. Whatever you feel about going back home, try to accept those feelings.

4. While you wait to visit, keep in touch with your family. Call, write, email. Use the new technology. This not only shows your children that you know how to learn new technologies, it shows them how much you value your family and your country of origin.

5. Acknowledge that when you are going back to visit, it is just that—a visit. It is temporary and it is not going home for good.

6. Remember to teach your children to love their roots. Talk to them about your country of origin and what they are likely to see, taste, smell, and experience when you arrive.

7. Be prepared for a flood of feelings when you return. The arrival back in America may rekindle some of the things you felt when you first came here or it may trigger some new, strong feelings.

8. Talk to your friends and family about what you are feeling, even if it's difficult to put into words.

9. Be prepared to answer questions your children may have about the differences and similarities between America and your country of origin, about why you decided to come here, and about why you are staying.

10. Remember that the ultimate goal is to balance both cultures—to be comfortable both here and there.

My Parenting Journal

When you reflect on the stories you read in this chapter, think about your own life and your own experiences, and how you can help your children find a balance between their love for their American country and their love for their heritage. Here are some questions to ponder.

1. How/What do I feel about going home for a visit?
2. If going home is not possible, what do I feel about not being able to go home? It may help to allow yourself to fantasize about what it would be like to go home. Think about the people you will see, the foods you will eat, the music you will hear. Such fantasies can be a comfort.
3. Have I taken the time to explain to my children why I came to this country and what benefits I have found here?
4. Have I talked about my childhood, my family, and the traditions of my native country?
5. Have I patiently answered all their questions about life over there versus life here, and why we are going home for a visit?
6. Have I made it clear that we will be coming back to America?

Chapter 9: From Boomers to Millennials: The Benefits of Being Bilingual and Bicultural

"To this day, my millennial sons thank me for helping them understand the importance of preserving our language and our customs, (i.e., black beans and rice with pork on Noche Buena/Christmas Eve). They are now reaping those benefits of a tradition, a language, and a culture that is engrained in their DNA and that I hope they pass on to their children."

—*Teresa Rodriguez, co-anchor, Univision's primetime award-winning weekly newsmagazine, Aquí y Ahora (Here and Now)*

What have been the benefits of being bilingual and bicultural for Baby Boomer parents and for the Millennial generation that has been raised in a multicultural society? In this chapter, I'd like to share the stories of parents and children who speak to this question in their own voices. It is my hope that the following stories will lift you up and encourage and motivate you further in your journey to raising bicultural children.

Betty Galván

Betty is a Mexican-American mother of three who grew up in Chicago. Her parents immigrated to the United States from Cuernavaca, Morelos, Mexico. Though her father is fluent in both English and Spanish, her mom can carry a conversation in English, but prefers to be known as a Spanish-speaker. Growing up, Betty was raised with Spanish at home: "My father prohibited us from speaking English in the house and would never consider himself or our family 'American.' Over the years, he has warmed up to the idea that he is more American than Mexican, but, to this day, we only speak Spanish at their house. Even to my kids, their grandkids, they only speak in Spanish."

When Betty was little, she didn't understand why her dad was so adamant about the language. But by the time she was old enough to rebel, she understood the importance of being fluent in two languages. She was also immersed in the culture. "We lived in a predominately Mexican neighborhood in Chicago, or right outside of Chicago, for a very long time. I didn't start to hang out with other races until I went to high school," she said. By then her dad worried that the American girls, or *guerritas*, would be a bad example and didn't favor Betty's friendships. She didn't agree with her dad, and she learned from her friendships: "I would say that seeing that there was no differences between my culture and others at an early age made me more open to learning about all cultures—and the travel bug bit!"

Before she traveled, there was school. Betty attended a predominately Latino high school in her hometown of Cicero, Illinois. She then went to being one of the few Mexican-American students majoring in English at Loyola University of Chicago in the year 2000. "When I applied, I most definitely identified as Latina," she said.

Betty believes that being fluent in both English and Spanish has always given her an advantage in the workforce: "Every job I ever had, from my first job at fifteen at a local candy store, which was owned by a white family and was a landmark in our town, to my first teaching position in a predominately Latino neighborhood, I have always used my Spanish speaking ability as an advantage."

Today Betty is the mother of three boys. They are being raised with two cultures. Teaching two languages is harder, but they try. "My boys are allowed to speak English at home. My oldest is eight and is fluent in Spanish. My four and three-year-olds are trying hard to speak in Spanish as often as possible. It is important for my husband and I that they learn to speak it fluently, but rather than forcing them the way my father did, we encourage it and have 'Spanish time' instead. My mother used to read to us in Spanish all the time and when I read to my boys, I think of those times. I want that for my kids, too," she said.

Though bilingualism is a challenge for the Galván family, they are working on it and committed to it. "My husband and I like to say that we are a third of the way to raising bilingual children. Another challenge is making sure our boys get enough Mexican culture in a community with no family and no Mexican influence. We do our best to teach our boys about our Mexican culture with books and travel," she said.

One way Betty and her husband teach the culture is through music. They listen to Mexican music and read Spanish books. And they tell the kids stories about their grandparents. "We still have family in Mexico and we want our children to know Mexico's contributions to the world and what fantastic people they are—hardworking and kind. We want them to be proud of their heritage," she said.

In addition to raising a family, Betty is the founder of MyFriendBettySays.com, a lifestyle blog for smart and stylish moms. "I have had an amazing opportunity to stay home with my boys when my husband and I decided to start a family," she said. "I decided to start blogging so that I could share my experiences as an expat mom in Japan back in 2007. My blogging has allowed me to start a different career and manage it all from my home office. I blog, freelance, work as an independent contractor, and a social media consultant. The majority of all my work goes back into the Latino community. Spanish is essential for all I do and I am so grateful for my bilingual abilities."

Betty added, "I believe that raising bicultural children teaches them to be more tolerant to other cultures and races. Bilingualism helps them open up their mind to different interests and travel, therefore leading to a world of endless possibilities. I would stress that it is imperative that parents support, encourage, and promote the importance of an education to their children. Latinos will need future generations to be prepared and well educated to take on major roles in society."

Victor and Julian Oquendo

Brothers Victor and Julian grew up in Miami, Florida. Their mom, Teresa Rodriguez, is a Spanish-language television personality who was born in Havana, Cuba, but was raised in Miami. Their father, Antonio Oquendo, was born in Santiago, Cuba. He came to the United States as a teenager. Both parents were raised bilingual, and they also raised their sons with two languages and two cultures.

"I grew up speaking both languages, and there was never a set language that we'd speak as a family. It depended on the situation and the setting. But I can tell that when my brother Julian and I got in trouble, the punishment was ALWAYS handed down in Spanish!" remembers Victor, the eldest of the two.

Julian agrees: "Yes, I remember that when speaking to my parents in the house, I would have to respond in Spanish, but when speaking to my brother or other friends, we would converse in English. My dad was strict about speaking in Spanish. As soon as he came home from work, we all spoke more Spanish than English. He would even engage my friends with the language, without realizing they didn't speak it. It was quite comical at times, especially when he would automatically speak in Spanish to my Lebanese friends!"

Because of their upbringing, Victor and Julian understand the importance of being bilingual and bicultural at a young age. Both parents worked for Univisión Network, and many of their friends were and are highly respected individuals within the Hispanic/Latino world in Miami. "As the oldest, I appreciated the advantages that came from being fluent in two languages," said Victor. "From advanced classes in school to real life situations making new friends or traveling in foreign countries where speaking Spanish was helpful in getting around and very helpful when getting my friends out of trouble."

It was harder for Julian. He wanted to be like his friends and speak English all the time. But he understood what his parents were doing. "One of the challenges of growing up in the U.S. as a Hispanic is that you go to English-speaking schools where school activities are all in English. If you do not have a strong language base at home, it can become very easy to lose the Spanish," he said.

In college, both brothers were able to use their second language to stand out. "I made a lot of friends in college because I overheard them speaking in Spanish in the dorms and I introduced myself," said Victor.

"I had a minor in Spanish so I used the Spanish courses as an outlet to speak Spanish amongst my peers for a couple of hours a week so that I could practice the language while I was away from home," said Julian.

"In my opinion," said Victor, "it has taken a while, but universities and businesses across the U.S. have finally realized how valuable diverse voices can be. In some cases, like my own, being bilingual is mandatory." Today, Victor is a news anchor and a reporter for ABC Affiliate, WPLG Local 10 News in Miami, and his ability to communicate in two languages has helped him conduct many important interviews in the language.

Julian agrees: "Most companies today seem to prefer a bilingual candidate over a monolingual applicant." Julian, who is pursuing a career in the music industry, believes that being bilingual and bicultural has prepared him for this time in his life. "I am on the verge of moving to Los Angeles and have been living in NYC for the past year. My experiences in New York have only been heightened by my fluency in Spanish and has opened doors for more connections. I anticipate the same will happen in LA."

Award-winning journalist mom, Teresa Rodriguez, also agrees: "My first job was at the local PBS affiliate in Miami. I was a bilingual reporter for a program, *The Nightly Business Report*, still on the air today. I was there for a few months when the CBS affiliate called me for a job interview, marking the beginning of a long and successful career in broadcast journalism. Being bilingual and bicultural was indeed an advantage."

Both brothers encourage the younger generations to never lose their heritage. "Our parents forced us to be fluent in both English and Spanish. And they taught us to love and appreciate both our Hispanic culture and our American culture. That is among the best thing they did for us," said Victor.

Jeannette Kaplun

Jeannette was born in El Paso, Texas, but her parents are from Chile. They are both bilingual, and she was raised with both English and

Spanish. Jeannette and her parents moved back to Chile when she was seven years old. She lived in Chile until she was twenty-four years old. "I was raised bilingual. When we lived in the U.S., my parents both spoke Spanish to me so I would learn it. When we moved to Chile, I attended an American school and my mom often spoke to me in English so I would practice. Back then, I was fortunate enough to visit the U.S. at least once a year during our summer vacations. My dad always preferred Spanish to English," she said.

All of Jeannette's schooling was in Chile. She obtained a bachelor's in social sciences from Universidad Gabriela Mistral and a bachelor's in mass communications and journalism from Pontificia Universidad Católica de Chile. "Truthfully, in Chile, they didn't care if I was bilingual or bicultural in college, but it made a huge difference when I was applying for internships and jobs. Being bilingual and bicultural set me apart from the rest. I always understood instinctively the importance of being both. I felt it allowed me to broaden my world, get to know more people and understand more cultures. I even took on a third language in high school, French, and loved it. I was pretty proficient and my first paying job while I was still in journalism school was adapting magazine articles from French into Spanish," she said.

Jeannette believes that the biggest reward has been the feeling that she is not limited by language. She works in both English and Spanish and navigates easily between cultures. But she understands that being bilingual can be challenging. There are things, words, and experiences that cannot be translated. "Sometimes your brain mixes up grammar or syntax. Even worse, sometimes you struggle for a few seconds to find the precise word in the other language. But I wouldn't change it for anything. That's why I am so adamant about raising my own kids to be bilingual and bicultural," she said.

Jeannette and her Peruvian-born husband have a twelve-year-old boy and a nine-year-old girl. They are both being raised bilingual and study Spanish in their schools. "Both our children speak English and Spanish fluently, and my son writes perfectly in Spanish. My daughter has a few issues with spelling, but she is younger, so it doesn't worry me. What

I love about watching them grow is that they are able to communicate with people from different cultures and seamlessly go from English to Spanish and vice-versa. My son, on his own, even gave a beautiful speech in Spanish for my father-in-law's seventy-fifth birthday," she said.

Education is key in her family. Jeannette and her husband always encourage their children to do well in school, to ask for help if they don't understand something, and the importance of obtaining a college degree. "The difference with my parents is that I am more involved in the day to day. When I was growing up, there was less homework and fewer school projects," she said.

Jeannette admits that keeping the children engaged and interested in learning Spanish is a challenge: "They prefer to speak English amongst themselves and their friends, even if their friends come from a Latino household. I keep trying to find fun ways to have them view a second language as something interesting and not a chore. Also, finding content that is culturally relevant is always a challenge."

During their vacation breaks, the family travels to Chile at least once a year. "It's a beautiful experience to see them appreciate the place you grew up in, taste the food you remember, and meet those you love. They also get to practice their Spanish and add new slang words to their vocabulary. They feel completely at home in Chile and even know the bad words! The worst part is always saying good-bye to my parents at the airport. The tears and hugs break my heart," she said.

Jeannette shares that having been raised with two languages and two cultures has made a difference in her professional life. "I have done TV in both languages, been published in both languages, and succeeded as a public speaker as well. I think being bilingual helps me adapt easier to different groups of people and audiences, which is key in today's business world." Today Jeannette is a journalist, television presenter, a top Latina blogger, and founder of HispanaGlobal.com, a website for the modern Hispanic woman.

Because she grew up appreciating her roots, she and her husband are making a conscious effort to expose their children to both Peruvian and Chilean history and culture. "It's part of who we are. We also share with them our European heritage," she said.

To parents of young children, Jeannette says, "Even though it's a challenge and very tiring at times, raising bilingual and bicultural children is worth the effort. Don't stop speaking your native language at home and lead by example. If you're proud of your heritage and show it, your kids will feel the same."

Gustavo Gutierrez

Gustavo is a young man born in Zacatecas, Mexico. His parents are both Mexicans from a small rural town called Los Reales, also in Zacatecas. His father is bilingual, and his mother understands English but is shy about speaking it. Spanish is her first language and how she likes to communicate.

Gustavo came to the United States when he was four years old. He was raised bilingual and bicultural. "My mother always spoke Spanish at home. My dad also spoke in Spanish, but there were times that he would speak to me in English. He said it was so he could sharpen his language abilities by practicing with me," he said.

However, both parents understood the importance of being fluent in both languages. "They would always say, '*En casa hablamos Español* (we speak Spanish at home); *y en la escuela hablan ingles* (in school you speak English.)'" And that is what they did. But it wasn't always easy. "I recall an instance over dinner when my siblings and I were talking in English and my dad immediately gave us that evil look that parents give when you have done something wrong. My mom was there, and he thought it was disrespectful to her that we weren't speaking in Spanish because she didn't understand English. In front of her, he prohibited us from speaking English. After that, my mom signed up for ESL classes. I think she felt bad that my dad was so mad at us!" he said.

Gustavo's mom learned enough English to get by, but Gustavo was her interpreter many times when they visited a doctor or when a letter would arrive. He credits his bilingualism to his parents' determination:

"I understood early on the rewards that being bilingual would bring to my life, and I appreciated my parents being strict about it."

Gustavo grew up in a predominantly Latino community. His friends were also bilingual and bicultural. He interacted with mostly Caucasian children at school. "These kids were in awe of my ability to communicate in two languages. They wanted to know more about me and how I was growing up with different experiences than the norm."

Gustavo considers himself Mexican-American. Mexican because he was born there, and American because he has spent close to ninety percent of his life here in the States and has grown up with many U.S. traditions. "I was raised bicultural because although we lived here in the U.S. and celebrated many American holidays and customs, we never forgot our rich Mexican traditions for the holidays. I come from a devoted Catholic family, so along with that came all the Catholic celebrations as well," he said. This means that his family celebrated *Las Posadas* and *Los Reyes Magos* (Three Kings Day) at Christmas, and that he was baptized and confirmed—typical Catholic traditions.

Gustavo believes that having been raised with two cultures has positively affected the way he lives his life: "I am a go-getter, a fighter, and a dreamer in big things. I believe that my parents didn't just bring us to this country just to see what happens, but to a great extent I have been influenced to make things happen. Being an immigrant to this country has helped me realize that I want to be different and fight the constant misconceptions that people have of Mexican immigrants— that we came here to take jobs away and that we are not educated."

Gustavo graduated with honors from high school. He then went off to Santa Clara University and received a bachelor's in communications. Then he received his master's in journalism from the University of Southern California, all the while using the fact that he was bilingual and bicultural because that was what made him different and unique. "I recall talking about my immigrant story and how I was a first-generation student when applying to college. That made my parents proud," he said.

Gustavo has had many career opportunities in the short years since graduating. He now manages marketing on a global basis for an international company. "At the different career opportunities that I have had, I have always brought up that I am bilingual/bicultural. A person like myself can relate to many people and different backgrounds. In the job force, we are understanding of others and employers want to see that," he said.

Being close to his family, Gustavo credits his sister for many of his accomplishments and his discipline: "Other than my parents, one other adult who has been an important influence in my life is my sister. My sister has been my role model, best friend, and lifelong supporter, and yes, she's Latina. I feel my sister has paved the way for me to follow her, to a great extent, in education and in being a successful entrepreneur. She's always been there for me to discuss my future plans and has always reminded me to do well to others, stay humble, and never forget where I come from."

For Gustavo's parents, it was easy to instill the love for his Mexican roots. "My parents helped me by showing how beautiful my people, my culture, food, music, and traditions were. We never lost our identity and my parents made sure that never happened. My father would always play the traditional *rancheras* and *corridos* music in the car and house. I enjoyed weekends because the music played loudly around the house, and it was always like a fiesta. We lived very humbly, but extremely happily. My father has always been a horse aficionado, so I always enjoyed going with him to watch rodeos, *coleaderos*, and a bunch of other traditional Mexican sports. To this day, we still go to rodeos together, and that is one of the best experiences because I get to connect with my father and have intellectual and deep conversations—just the two of us," he said.

Gustavo believes that being bilingual and bicultural opens up many opportunities for him to choose from: "I've learned to really appreciate the smallest things and not take my opportunities here in the States for granted. When you have dreams and aspirations, there's absolutely nothing and nobody who could kill them—only the mind of a pessimist. To be fluent in more than one language and to be bicultural is the new cool thing. My career has benefitted because I am diverse in so many aspects, and I am able to bring that to any office or meeting that I may be a part of. I love my Mexican heritage so much!"

"I know firsthand what it's like to be bi-cultural," she says, "I am a child of two worlds. Born in Houston, my parents are both from El Salvador, where I grew up. I came to the United States to attend college. My dual heritage allowed me the opportunity to work as a television and entertainment producer and content creator, with a specialty in the U.S. Hispanic industry, both in the U.S. and in Mexico. Since then, I have been able to use both my bilingualism and my being bicultural to succeed as a published author and social media strategist and influencer. I want the same opportunities for my daughter."

- Ana L. Flores, founder of *Latina Bloggers Connect* and We All Grow Summit and co-author of the book, *Bilingual is Better.*

Marinés Arroyo-Sotomayor

Of all the stories I have shared in this chapter, Marinés's story is a bit different. Like me, Marinés is Puerto Rican, and her parents are both Puerto Ricans. She grew up monolingual, speaking only Spanish at home. Her mom is the more bilingual one of her parents. She speaks and understands some English, but also grew up with monolingual Spanish, as did Marinés's father. Born in the city of Ponce, Marinés grew up in Jayuya, speaking only Spanish.

Marinés studied in Puerto Rico until her third year of college. It was then that she went to Illinois as an exchange student, where she polished her knowledge of the English language. She went back to the island for her fourth year and graduated with a degree in public communications. By then, Marinés was completely bilingual. She then decided to continue her education in Florida, where she obtained a master's degree in investigative journalism.

"When I applied for jobs after my schooling, I always included that I was bilingual," she said. "I worked for a company that mainly communicated in English at the corporate level. For my first job in

AOL Latino, I had to be able to write in both languages."

Though her plan was to come to the U.S. to study and then go back to the island, Marinés was offered a job after she graduated and ended up staying here. She now has three children, all born in the States. "My kids are being raised with two languages," she said. "We speak Spanish at home and my oldest gets the English at school. My little ones hear Spanish all the time. They are not in school yet."

In addition to the language, to nurture her Hispanic culture, Marinés takes her kids to visit Puerto Rico every summer to eat the traditional foods. "But to me, being fluent in Spanish is the most important thing. When my oldest son started school at two years old, he started to forget some Spanish. The constant interaction with teachers and classmates made it easy for him to choose English. With time, it became more difficult, so I started to change things to practice the language," she said. Now when Marinés and her son are alone, especially in the car, driving to and from school, she finds opportunities to speak in Spanish. "I bring basics things into the conversation like the days of the week. And I ask him to say the words he knows in Spanish so I can hear the sound. I love the way he sounds when he speaks Spanish, but he feels self-conscious, so we are working on that." The family also has implemented "Spanish moments" when going on walks. Her son also practices Spanish with a Spanish DVD set and books that his grandmother gave him.

Marinés is teaching her two sons and her daughter to love the Spanish language for cultural reasons, but also because she believes it will provide more career advantages in the future: "My son already understands that being fluent in both languages could make a difference in getting a job over others, especially in Florida."

Formerly a managing editor for HuffPost Voces, Marinés is taking some time off to raise her three children. "College prepared me for a bilingual world, but I was lucky enough to learn some basic English in the Puerto Rican public school system," she said. "It has helped my career path and I am grateful for that."

Rocio's Story: Undocumented, she Finds a Cultural Balance and Conquers it All

Rocio was born in a small town in Mexico called Tepatlaxco de Hidalgo. Both her parents are from the same town. Rocio came to the United States at six years old, and she still remembers the experience. "When I was crossing the border, my name was Jackie. I had this pretty pink dress on, and my uncle, who was helping me cross, thought it was not American enough, so he tossed it and dressed me in pants, a t-shirt, and sneakers," she said. Rocio recalls not being able to sleep for days because she was so afraid she would never see her mom again. But she did. Once the family reunited, they began their new life in America. From that moment on, she was raised bilingual and bicultural.

Rocio's parents are monolingual and only speak Spanish at home, while she learned English at school. But the English language was hard for her, and she felt ashamed of her heavy accent, especially when she was asked to read out loud. Learning the grammar was also difficult. But she was determined to study hard, get good grades, and go to college, regardless of the hardships brought on by her undocumented status.

Rocio's memories of the early years include a combination of disappointing situations and prideful moments. As a young child, she was her dad and uncle's English language translator. Her dad would tell her in Spanish what he wanted communicated to his bosses, and in her best English, she would tell them. "There were many times where I would be pressured and scolded by my dad and uncle if I didn't know the proper terminology, or failed to communicate the correct message. At times, I would be told, 'Why are you even going to school, don't they teach you good English there?!' Out of respect, I would remain silent and just remember to try harder next time," she said. She is still her dad's translator today, but now understands why her father and uncle needed her help. Like her, Rocio's dad was undocumented and she believes he was abused verbally and taken advantage of because of his status. "I came to realize this when there was one time I was translating for Papa, that his 'boss' started yelling at me because, according to him, my father was not doing his job. My father had reassured him that it wasn't his fault, but that his boss's request had been lost in translation. At that moment, I wanted to tell his boss off and protect my father from abuse with the only way I could: my English. I came to appreciate my father's bravery in not giving up and still being able to bring money to the house without any English," she said.

As a young girl, she had an understanding of being bicultural and bilingual. She was learning to live in America, but she still spoke, ate, celebrated, and lived as a proud Mexicana. She lived in East Los Angeles where the majority of the population was Latino. The traditions were still the same as the ones in Mexico, and the people she saw on a daily basis were the same ethnicity as her. "I only felt different when I went to school and I was called out to read out loud for the entire class. This was my nightmare and shame throughout my elementary and middle school years," she said.

But then things changed in high school. She got involved with the arts and her pride soared. "I decided to come out of the shadows during my senior year to tell the whole entire school my true identity. I decided to participate in the performing arts program and began writing poems that narrated who I was. The first time during rehearsals, I broke down because it hit me. From then on, I decided to gain some strength and courage to reveal my biggest weakness to the entire school." Rocio believes that this experience helped her gain pride and respect, and she became unashamed of her background. "From that point on, I figured that the arts was my form of being outspoken. I came to realize that it was no time to be scared and fearful, when I clearly had people that understood my struggle and commended me for being brave. I forever thank the arts for helping me develop pride for my culture, and teaching me how to love myself," she said. Through the arts, she was also able to help her mom financially by making colorful bracelets and scarfs, and selling them at school or at an arts program center in Los Angeles, where she developed as an artist.

At her high school graduation, Rocio was valedictorian of her class.

But, because of her undocumented status, she was not able to attend a college of her dreams. The Dream Act was not enacted yet, and her mother was not supportive of Rocio pursuing a higher education. The family couldn't help her financially. She then decided she was going to do it alone. She enrolled at California State University, Los Angeles, and majored in theatre. "My fear of failing and not pursuing my dreams became my strongest strategies," she said. "I began to save. I took action rather than allowing my fear to win. I managed to receive scholarships, fundraised to pay for my own college tuition, and I began to work. And because I was determined, that gave me the understanding and the level of communication that I needed to communicate with my parents at a much higher level. Like making my mother understand that I didn't have the time to help her clean anymore and asked her to give me the support I needed academically." And her parents are very proud of her. She is the first in her family to achieve a higher education.

Rocio believes that having people cheering you on and encouraging you along the way can also make a difference. In her case, she is thankful for her history teacher in high school who was always there to listen to her and offer advice, guidance, and motivation. "Not only did he pay for my senior packet, but he was always there for me like a dad, pushing me to become the best. He believed in my maturity and potential, and always reminded me how unique I was as a human being. At times, when he understood how much harder my journey was going to be because I was undocumented, he would always end his final sentences with, 'You will be okay.' And 'you will be okay' is what keeps me going. I am forever grateful to him," she said.

When I asked Rocio what makes her most proud of her culture, she quickly says "food." She said her mother and aunt are excellent cooks, and they always make typical dishes for visiting friends who fall in love with the food. "My mother, aunt, and entire family never let our traditions down in order to assimilate entirely to the American culture. From *Los Reyes Magos*, to *El Dia Del Los Niños*, to *the Day of the Dead*, from celebrating *Las Virgen De Guadalupe's Mañanitas*, to *Celebrating our*

Santos, our traditions are what made me prideful and knowledgeable about my culture," she said.

Rocio believes that being bilingual and bicultural is an advantage. Latinos have become the largest population in this country and speaking Spanish is a sought-out job requirement. "Being bilingual and bicultural has benefitted me in so many ways, like in my career as a theater major, and now as a young playwright. I am able to write in Spanglish because that's the culture I like to write about. Although I am able to tell a story in English, I'm able to express myself and educate the audience with an undocumented culture. And in my future career, I would like to focus on telling the undocumented stories through theater," she said.

In addition to her theater work, Rocio also works at the Dreamers Resource Center at California State University, Los Angeles (CSULA.) In this job, she represents and inspires other undocumented students to take a stand on being undocumented and become educated. She said, "At this point in my life and through my job, I feel responsible to represent those who are still struggling in the shadows, letting them know that they are not alone."

Rocio's message for millennial Latinos: "Never let your status define or limit how high you can dream. If you want it, chase it, and stay focused, know that anything is possible. Live life with this quote, 'The most common way people give up their power is by thinking they don't have any.' (Alice Walker). Don't ever let anyone tell you 'no'. Yes, know that people like us have to work twice or three times as hard, but eventually, we become the brightest stars in the universe. We are a unique group of people that will work nonstop to get what we want. Know that one can, and know that many have. Because when one believes and whispers to themselves, 'Yes I can... You can and you will!'"

Pocket Sun: A Non-Latina Shares Her Immigrant Story

Yiqing (Pocket) Sun was born in a small city in Northern China called Dongying. Her parents are from two different provinces in China. They only speak Mandarin. Pocket was raised monolingual, speaking Mandarin at home. She learned English in middle and high school. By the time Pocket went to college in the United States, she was bilingual, but not bicultural.

"I first came to the U.S. at eighteen and went to a white college with very few Chinese students," she said. "At first, I had a hard time understanding people's expressions. Words such as 'outfit', 'awesome', or 'gross' were not taught in my textbooks back in China. I didn't understand abbreviations such as 'cu', 'lol' or 'gr8'. Overall, I was a FOB (fresh off the boat) who made numerous mistakes because of the language barrier. I was not able to tell if guys were being friendly or showing affection. I had no choice but to fit in the environment because my college was at least 70 percent white. What helped me was joining different clubs and organizations to have close interactions with local students."

In the States, she lived in Virginia, Chicago, and Los Angeles, and she went all the way to graduate school. She has a bachelor's degree in marketing and a master's degree in entrepreneurship and innovation. She believes that being bilingual has opened many doors and that learning American culture has also contributed to her career success.

"I have done really well as a foreigner because I built an organization that is very appealing to people from all over the world. My event attendees are always very diverse and international," she said. Yet her parents continue to encourage pride in her heritage. "I am very proud to be Chinese. I am breaking many stereotypes Americans have for Chinese people."

Pocket travels back to China once or twice a year, depending on her schedule: "China is changing very rapidly, so every time I feel the difference and I am impressed by my country's development. I wouldn't mind living in China, but my boyfriend (a white American) does not want to. Therefore, we are moving to Singapore together. I miss the food! I miss my family the most."

When asked about her bicultural experience so far, she said, "Many bicultural kids grow up hating their cultural identity. They have a lot of identity issues and feel that they cannot fit in with American kids. They want to become more like the white kids, but white kids don't like hanging out with them anyways. I wish more people could be more aware of the issue and encourage diversity and inclusivity."

These days Pocket is a very busy entrepreneur. She is the founder of SoGal and founding partner of SoGal Ventures, the first female-led Millennial venture capital firm investing in diverse funding teams in both the U.S. and Asia. In less than a year, Pocket has created a global community for emerging female entrepreneurs and investors in twenty-six countries. Her next step is to establish the first Millennial cross-border venture capital fund to invest in young, diverse entrepreneurs in the U.S. and Asia.

"Being bilingual and bicultural is fortunate. I feel that there are so many gaps I can bridge and so many business opportunities that only people like me can take on. My goal is to build a business empire between the U.S. and Asia," she said.

My Own Story

I was born and raised in Puerto Rico, and I came to study in the United States when I was twenty-one years old. When I came to live in California, I learned to live with two cultures. When I got married to a Greek-American a few years later, the Greek culture was added to my everyday life. As a Baby Boomer mom who raised children with three different cultures, I believe that my Millennial children's multiculturalism has taught them to be tolerant, respectful, compassionate, and understanding of all individuals in the global society they call home. There are no words that express how enriched my life has been as a multicultural person.

My kids have grown up appreciating three cultures and feel pride in their heritages. My son has his own business and though he doesn't need his Spanish every day, he is able to converse with Spanish-speaking people who call his office. He also speaks with my parents often, and always in Spanish. He is very connected to his Hispanic culture and enjoys visiting my family and all the customs that entails. He loves the food, the music, and being able to say, "I am fifty percent Puerto Rican!" He is also proud of his Greek heritage and believes that having been raised with multiple cultures helps him be himself: "It's not about here or there, your flag or my flag, your culture, my culture. It's about being able to express yourself as you see fit in a way that is grounded in compassion and self-awareness."

My daughter is in her last year of college and she is studying abroad in Spain. A seasoned traveler, she is very comfortable living with a family that speaks to her in Spanish all the time and is enjoying the experience and the opportunity to learn more about her Spanish ancestors and roots. Equally important, she is excited at the prospect of coming back home and applying for jobs where she can stand out because of her bilingualism and multiculturalism.

Maria Cristina Marrero, who offered her comments earlier, echoes the sentiment: "As a Millennial, I feel like I'm in a sweet spot compared to my counterparts because I have a bicultural approach, as well as a global mentality. Companies these days are more aware of the different markets; they want to target those markets. My expertise in both the American and the Hispanic culture is without a doubt an advantage."

Ana L. Flores, founder of Latina Bloggers Connect and co-author of the book, *Bilingual is Better*, also agrees: "The ability to communicate in both Spanish and English is extremely useful in being able to compete in the 21st century business world. Today, it's undeniable that being bilingual or multilingual in any combination of languages is a valuable life skill that opens up cognitive, cultural and professional doors."

For Teresa Rodriguez, a boomer and a Cuban immigrant who came to the United States when she was nine months old, speaking a second language was not just something she did out of the desire to fit in; it was a necessity. Her first exposure to English was via television and radio, followed by preschool classes and classmates. Her father spoke broken English, and her mom only learned a few words. This meant that at a very young age, she became the official translator in her home. And though she was quickly learning about her new culture, her parents had a strict rule about language: Spanish was the only language spoken at home, and English was spoken at school and among her friends. "Although I didn't quite agree with their tactics, now I thank them for not allowing me to forget our vibrant, colorful language and culture. Looking back, they were absolutely right—being bilingual was certainly advantageous in a competitive market place, not to mention that NEVER in my wildest dreams could I have imagined that I would make my livelihood as a journalist with a Spanish-language television network!"

Our world has become global and very much multicultural. Social media has allowed us to have easy access to people around the world, and that is contributing to our commitment of raising multicultural children. More than ever before, parents are making every effort to encourage their children to not only learn a second language, but also travel to places that speak the language of choice for their education. College and universities have also increased their study abroad programs, and there is a concentrated effort to ensure that studying abroad is part of a student's academic four-year course schedule. The internet is filled with resources to help and guide parents in their quest to instill a love for their multiple heritages and for bilingualism. Today, more and more dual immersion schools have emerged in many states across the country, and Caucasian parents are among those advocating and supporting these programs. There is not one day that goes by that social media doesn't highlight another young Latino female or male who is making a difference as an entrepreneur or as part of an American company, reaffirming the benefits of being raised bilingual and bicultural!

> "Being bicultural has allowed me the opportunity to travel the world and feel comfortable speaking in two languages and learning about other cultures and share mine. I have lived in Spain, in Argentina, and in Miami. I navigate easily between the two cultures and that has been a great advantage in my career."
>
> - Maria Cristina Marrero, a millennial, Vice President Editorial, Hola USA

Tips for Raising Bicultural Children

By now, you have read many of the tips mentioned in other chapters and if you are a parent, you will consider using them to raise bicultural children. If you are a not a parent yet, I am hoping you will read these tips again when the time comes. In the meantime, here are a few more suggestions.

1. Why are you proud of your heritage? Why is it important to you that your children feel that pride?
2. Have you stuck to the plan of action to instill pride in your native country?
3. If your kids were born in the United States, were you able to maintain speaking the native language at home? Were you strict and consistent?
4. Did you keep an open communication with your kids about the two cultures and were you understanding about this pull for one culture over another? Did you allow them to share their feelings about the two cultures?
5. Did you involve your family in both cultures from the beginning? Did you make it part of everyday life by celebrating

both customs and traditions?

6.   If you are a young adult, did your parents succeed in raising you to love the two cultures? Will you do the same when you are a parent?

My Parenting Journal

I am hoping that by including this section in each chapter, I've given you the opportunity to reflect on your adjustment to the new culture. Whether you are a parent now or will be a parent in the future, here are some questions that might help you evaluate your bicultural journey.

1.   As an immigrant parent, have I succeeded in my quest to help my children feel proud of their heritage?

2.   Have I been a positive role model for my children as it relates to tolerance and respect for other cultures?

3.   Have I been open to the possibility that my children might identify more with the American culture rather than my native culture?

4.   Have I been able to find a balance and embrace my children's mixed heritages?

5.   Have I been willing to learn about the American culture and appreciate my life here?

Final Thoughts

Blending two cultures is a journey. Most immigrants will remain with one foot here and the other foot there for a very long time; some for always. It is a difficult path, requiring patience and faith. To achieve it, build a personal support system, take advantage of local resources, and build a relationship with your children. Today there are so many resources to help with the transition and many of them are accessible via the internet. Websites like http://mamasporelmundo.com/—a consulting company that provides support and counseling to expatriate women and their families as they face their lives in a new country. Laura Garcia and Erica Mirochnik, professional experts and expat moms themselves, provide a vast array of services covering practical issues like choosing a school, learning a new language, and adapting to a new culture. They also help families in facing the emotional issues of the expatriation, like living far from friends and family, and coping with the strain of adaptation to a new environment. Other websites/blogs like "Unknownmami" by Claudya Martinez, provide a perspective from a bilingual Latina mom raising multicultural children. And since language can help instill pride in the culture, there are websites like "Bilingual Avenue", founded by Marianna Du Bosq. In this site, and via weekly podcasts, Du Bosq offers tips, resources, tools, and guidance for raising bilingual children.

Friends and family can help, too. Often times, family members come here before we do, and they can offer assistance, suggestions, and guidance. At work or at our children's school, we make friends who can also help with the transition.

As I mentioned in the first chapter, it is important for the adults that emigrate here to adjust to their new life before they can help their children adjust. And even though there are times when we as adults don't assimilate completely, our children tend to rather quickly.

We should embrace that and continue instilling the sense of Latino/ Hispanic pride.

When we feel comfortable with our American friends, when we walk into a conference room to give a presentation and see our colleagues as peers, when we go for a job interview and answer comfortably in English, then we can say we have arrived. When we are able to walk into our child's school and be an advocate for our child's education, when we celebrate our Latino traditions along with the American holidays, when we watch *telenovelas* on Spanish language television and the news in English, we have reached the final stage of immigrant adjustment, the acceptance stage; the stage that makes sense, that balances our lives, and where we feel comfortable eating either *arroz con pollo* or apple pie.

Finally, as you feel more at home in your new country, consider helping those who have just emigrated. When a new immigrant arrives, invite them and their kids over to your house. Share your immigrant experience with them. Offer advice, tips, and suggestions that might help make the transition easier for the family. Become a resource for that family, and introduce them to other immigrant parents who have successfully achieved cultural integration. Sometimes, all it takes is a friendly face reminding you that, someday, you will feel comfortable eating *Arroz con Pollo* AND *Apple Pie!*

Resources

Books

- *Bilingual is Better,* by Ana L. Flores and Roxana A. Soto (Sept. 2012)
- *Enrique's Journey,* by Sonia Nazario, (Random House, 2007)
- *Latina Power!* Using 7 Strengths You Already Have to Create the Success You Deserve by Dr. Ana Nogales (Touchstone, September 16, 2003)
- *No Birthday for Mara, Tristan Wolf, The Wanting Monster* by Mariana Llanos http://www.marianallanos.com/#!books/c44h
- *Raising Nuestros Niños* by Gloria Rodriguez, Ph.D. (Fireside, May 26, 1999)
- *Becoming Naomi León* by Pam Muñoz Ryan (Scholastic, 2004)
- *Rubber Shoes/Los Zapatos de Goma, Pink Fire Trucks/Los*
- *Camiones de Bomberos de Color Rosado, and Monster Slayer/ Exterminadora de monstruos* by Gladys Elizabeth Barbieri (Big Tent Books, 2011,2013, 2016)
- *Freaky Foods from Around the World/Platillos Sorprendentes de todo el Mundo and The Wooden Bowl/El bol de Madera* by Ramona Moreno Winner (Brainstorm 3000, 2005,2009)
- *Loteria, Zapata, Frida and Guadalupe by Patty Rodriguez and Ariana Stein* (Lil'Libros, 2013) http://www.lillibros.com/

Websites/Blogs

- Multicultural Familia (www.multiculturalfamilia.com/ multicultural-families-resources-directory/)
- Mamás por el mundo (www.mamasporelmundo.com/)
- Kid World Citizen (www.kidworldcitizen.org)

- Mama Smiles (www.mamasmiles.com/exploring-geography/)
- Explor-A-World Language and Culture Programs (www.exploraworld.org)
- De Su Mama (www.desumama.com)
- Bicultural Mama (www.BiculturalMama.com)
- En Tus Zapatos (www.facebook.com/entuszapatosblog/?fref=ts)
- Bilingual Avenue (www.bilingualavenue.com/)
- Unknownmami (www.unknownmami.com/)
- Mommymaestra (www.mommymaestra.com/)
- Mommyteaches (www.mommyteaches.com/)
- Myfriendbettysays (www.myfriendbettysays.com/)
- MamiTalks (www.mamitalks.com/)
- Growing Up Bilingual (www.growingupbilingual.com/)
- La Familia Cool (www.lafamiliacool.com/)
- One Latina Mom (www.onelatinamom.com/)
- Multilingual Parenting (www.multilingualparenting.com/)

Print Media/Online magazines

- *Ser Padres* (www.serpadres.com/)
- *Parents Latina* (www.parents.com/parents-latina-magazine/)
- *Todobebé* (www.todobebe.com/)
- *HipLatina* (www.hiplatina.com/)

Organizations & Websites

- Center for Public Education (www.centerforpubliceducation.org/)
- Families in Schools (www.familiesinschools.org/)
- National Association for Bilingual Education (www.nabe.org/)
- Parent Teacher Association (www.pta.org/)

- EBInternacional.org (www.ebinternacional.org/)
- UC Undocumented Student Services (www.undoc.universityofcalifornia.edu/campus-support.html)
- On Raising Bilingual Children (www.onraisingbilingualchildren.com/)
- California Association for Bilingual Education (www.bilingualeducation.org/)

Bilingual Schools for young children
- Spanish in Action (www.spanishinaction.com/)
- Mi Escuelita (www.myescuelita.com/)
- Bilingual Birdies (www.bilingualbirdies.com/NYC/)
- Spanish Horizons (www.spanishhorizons.com)

Acknowledgments

This book would have not been published without the help and support of the many wonderful people in my life. To Leo Estrada, my wise friend, Thank You for believing in me and for being there every step of the way. To everyone who shared their immigrant stories with me, I owe you a debt of gratitude. Thank You for your trust! I want to believe that the world is a better place because you told your story! To everyone that offered a comment or an insight, Thank You for your participation.

To my writing coach and editor Jennie Nash, Thank You for believing in my project, for seeing its potential, and for all the great insights and suggestions. To Ana Nogales, Thank You for your support and your care, and for being the first to promote this book through Doctora Ana magazine a few years ago! To Connie Spenuzza (aka Cecilia Velástegui), for your kindness, support, encouragement, and, mostly, your selfless generosity. You inspire me!

To Marcela Landres, thanks for all the comments and suggestions to my original manuscript. To Nora Comstock and Las Comadres organization, thanks for all your support. To Caroline Griswold, Thank You for taking the time to read the manuscript and giving me your millennial insights! To Nikos Bellas and Kaitlan Mattern, I'm so very grateful for your help with the book cover design, the last minute manuscript editing, formatting, and proofreading. Your unwavering assistance and organization made a huge difference! Thank You!

To my Latina friends and mothers: Ivelisse Estrada, Monica Lozano, Magali Vitale, Cecilia Grosso, Yvonne Turner, Ana Barbosa and Maria Contreras Sweet, I am grateful for your encouragement and unconditional love. To my "comadre" Alycia Enciso, thanks for your friendship and continuous support. A heartfelt Thank You to all the Latina bloggers I have met through Latina Bloggers Connect

154

and Latinas Think Big. You have been a source of empowerment and inspiration!

To my American friends and mothers: Bridget Batkin, Mary Klem, Audrey Alfano, Martha Kretzmer, Lisa Guidone, Andrea Utley, Ellie Allman, and Jill Latimer, it has been an honor to walk the motherhood journey with you all these years. You taught me to value and respect the American way!

To Stephanie Kracht, Thank You for taking the time to help me develop my vision for what the book cover should look like. You are an amazing artist!

I am grateful to my sister, Marisol, the most amazing mom I know, for dropping everything when I called to ask if she would do the Spanish version of this book and for managing my social media platforms! And for being there when I need her! You are my hero!!

To my parents, Teté and Gilberto, Thank You for teaching me to love passionately and unconditionally, and to be proud of my Hispanic roots. To my in-laws, Akri and Gus, no longer with us, but the most beautiful Greek-Americans I ever knew. They taught me the value of immigrant pride.

To my children, Nikos and Franceska, you are my EVERYTHING... I hope this book inspires you to raise your children bilingual AND bicultural and to never forget where you came from! Last but not least, to my husband, Peter. You are the wind beneath my wings. Thanks for believing in me.

ABOUT THE AUTHOR

Born and raised in Puerto Rico, Maritere Rodriguez Bellas is both bilingual and bicultural. As an author and writer, she has been a voice of Latino immigrant parents for two decades.

Maritere has been a featured writer in *La Opinión*, *Ser Padres*, Huffpost, HipLatina, Todobebé, and Mamasporelmundo. She writes for immigrant parents and regularly shares her expertise as a seasoned Latina mom on Spanish language media. Her first book, *Raising Bilingual Children* was published in English and Spanish in 2014. She lives with her family in California.

To learn more about Maritere Rodriguez Bellas, please visit:
www.maritererodriguezbellas.com

Made in the USA
Lexington, KY
24 February 2017